TUNISIA

PROFILES • NATIONS OF THE CONTEMPORARY MIDDLE EAST
Bernard Reich and David E. Long,
Series Editors

Tunisia: Crossroads of the Islamic and European Worlds
Kenneth J. Perkins

Algeria: The Revolution Institutionalized, John P. Entelis

Israel: Land of Tradition and Conflict, Bernard Reich

The Republic of Lebanon: Nation in Jeopardy, David C. Gordon

Jordan: Crossroads of Middle Eastern Events, Peter Gubser

South Yemen: A Marxist Republic in Arabia, Robert W. Stookey

Syria: Modern State in an Ancient Land, John F. Devlin

Turkey: Coping with Crisis, George S. Harris

The Sudan: Unity and Diversity in a Multicultural State,
John Obert Voll and Sarah Potts Voll

Libya: Qadhafi and the Green Revolution, Lillian Craig Harris

The United Arab Emirates: A Venture in Unity,
Malcolm C. Peck

Iran: At War with History, John W. Limbert

Afghanistan: Marx, Mullah, and Mujahid, Ralph H. Magnus

Bahrain: The Modernization of Autocracy, Fred Lawson

Oman, Calvin H. Allen, Jr.

North Yemen, Manfred W. Wenner

ABOUT THE BOOK AND AUTHOR

Tunisia's location at the middle of Africa's Mediterranean coast and at the edge of the Sahara has made the exposure of its people to the cultures of the Middle East, Europe, and Africa inevitable. Indeed, Tunisia has often been a conduit for the passage of ideas from one of these regions to another.

Of all the influences that have helped shape modern Tunisian society, however, two stand out: the country's enduring commitment to Islam and its extensive contacts with Europe culminating in three-quarters of a century of French rule from 1881 to 1956. After considering these factors in an overview of Tunisian history, Professor Perkins examines the country's political and governmental structures and the role of Habib Bourguiba and other nationalist leaders in molding those institutions and in controlling them since independence. He also focuses on the process of extensive social and economic change since 1956 that has dramatically altered Tunisian society and affected the lives of all Tunisians.

The book concludes with a study of Tunisia's foreign policy, stressing the country's status as a small state surrounded by more powerful, less moderate nations. Tunisia's handling of such regional issues as the Arab-Israeli problem and the upsurge of Islamic fundamentalism is considered, as are its relations with the superpowers and its European and African neighbors.

Kenneth J. Perkins is associate professor of history at the University of South Carolina. He is the author of *Qaids, Captains, and Colons: French Military Administration in the Colonial Maghrib, 1844–1930* (1981) and translator of *On the Eve of Colonialism: North Africa Before the French Conquest, 1790–1830* by Lucette Valensi (1977).

TUNISIA

Crossroads of the Islamic and European Worlds

Kenneth J. Perkins

Westview Press • Boulder, Colorado

Croom Helm • London and Sydney

The cover photo of a 1952 Tunisian postage stamp depicts an arabesque design from the interior of the Grand Mosque in Kairouan. Tunisia's political status as a French protectorate is suggested by the RF (République Française) monogram in the upper right-hand corner and the Tunisian national symbol of the crescent moon and star in the upper left-hand corner.

Copyright © 1986 by Westview Press, Inc.

Published in 1986 in the United States of America by Westview Press, Inc.; Frederick A. Praeger, Publisher; 5500 Central Avenue, Boulder, Colorado 80301

Published in 1986 in Great Britain by Croom Helm Ltd., Provident House, Burrell Row, Beckenham, Kent, BR3 1AT

Library of Congress Cataloging-in-Publication Data
Perkins, Kenneth J.
   Tunisia : crossroads of the Islamic and European worlds.
   (Profiles/Nations of the contemporary Middle East)
   Bibliography: p.
   Includes index.
   1. Tunisia.   I. Title.   II. Series: Profiles.
Nations of the contemporary Middle East.
DT245.P47   1986   961'.1   86-5590
ISBN 0-86531-591-4 (alk. paper)

British Library Cataloging in Publication Data
Perkins, Kenneth J.
   Tunisia: crossroads of the Islamic and European worlds.
(Profiles: nations of the contemporary Middle East)
   1. Tunisia—history.
   I. Title
   961'.1   DT254
ISBN 0-7099-4050-5

Printed and bound in the United States of America

The paper used in this publication meets the requirements of the American National Standard for Permanence of Paper for Printed Library Materials Z39.48-1984.

10   9   8   7   6   5   4   3   2   1

Contents

Illustrations

A Note on Transliteration

Personal names and terms in Arabic have been transliterated throughout this book without the use of diacritical marks or the symbols normally used to indicate sounds not found in English. Nonspecialists often find these orthographic symbols confusing; specialists will recognize the words without them.

In the case of Tunisian cities (Sousse, Bizerte, and Sfax, for example) and also in the case of Tunisia's president, Habib Bourguiba, standard Western spellings have been used in lieu of the more technically correct, but less recognizable, formal transliterations.

Northern Africa and the Middle East

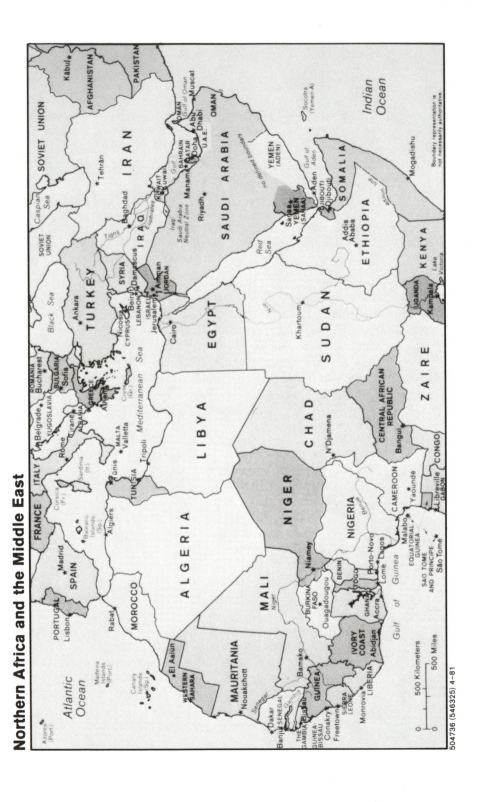

504736 (546325) 4-81

1

Land and People

Tunisia lies in the center of the North African coastline, almost equidistant from the Nile Valley and the Atlantic Ocean. The Mediterranean shoreline of Africa, which runs more or less due east from the Atlantic, turns abruptly south at Tunisia, giving the country two faces on the Mediterranean, one to the north toward Europe and a second to the east toward the Arabo-Islamic heartlands. These two regions have exerted the most significant influences on Tunisia, often in competition with each other. Tunisia's northeastern extremity, the Cape Bon peninsula, defines the approximate midpoint of the Mediterranean Sea. The narrow strait between the peninsula and the Italian island of Sicily links the eastern and western halves of the sea. Tunisia's proximity to this chokepoint has given it strategic importance in recent years.

The country extends south from the Mediterranean for some 500 miles, and its average east-west width is approximately 150 miles, giving it an area of 63,378 square miles. Tunisia shares borders with Algeria on the west and Libya on the east. The absence of any natural geographical dividing lines between Tunisia and its neighbors has created political problems in the postcolonial era and historically often drew the territory that is now Tunisia into larger geopolitical units extending well beyond its present borders.

Tunisia's climate is typically Mediterranean, with warm, dry summers and cool, moist winters prevailing everywhere except in the south. The considerable range of elevations in the country, with the land generally falling away from west to east, influences temperatures and precipitation. The highlands in western Tunisia are the easternmost extension of the Atlas mountain range, which begins in Morocco and continues across all North Africa. Tunisia's other major geographic feature, the Sahara, is part of the great desert stretching from the Atlantic Ocean to the Red Sea.

1

Tunisia encompasses three quite distinct geographical regions determined by their physical features and amounts of rainfall. The Tell lies north of the Dorsal, a mountain chain extending from the Algerian border to Cape Bon. It receives an average minimum of 16 inches of rain per year, with some areas in the extreme northwest having as much as 36 inches annually. The Tell is generally described as a coastal plain, but the land is not flat, and much of it consists of rolling hills and low mountains. In the northwest, large stands of cork and oak forests cover much higher mountains. More densely populated than other portions of the country, the Tell contains the best soil in Tunisia, especially in the Majarda Valley, through which the country's only significant perennial river flows. Agriculture has thrived in the Tell since ancient times. The Romans cultivated cereal there, as did the French and other European settlers who came to Tunisia in the nineteenth and twentieth centuries. More recently, olives have been introduced to the Tell from other parts of the country, and citrus and truck farming have developed in the areas around Tunis and Bizerte.

Stretching south from the Dorsal to a line of hills near Gafsa are the Steppes, a semiarid region subdivided from west to east into the High Steppes, the Low Steppes, and the Sahil along the coast. The Sahil area is heavily populated and cultivated because of its sandy soil, substantial supply of underground water, and average rainfall of as much as 20 inches a year. Included in the Sahil area are the island of Jarba and the Qarqanna (Kerkenna on map) Islands. This region, more than any other in the country, has always been open to outside influences. Unlike regions farther north and south, no natural barriers prevented the penetration of this attractive environment. Rain is less plentiful in the High and Low Steppes, ranging from 14 inches in the north to as little as 7 inches in the south. Limited agriculture is possible in the Low Steppes, and the region around Kairouan produces olives, citrus fruits, and some cereals. Cereal cultivation is much riskier on the High Steppes; as a result, farming is less common and nomadism was the dominant way of life until quite recently.

Desert terrain covers the southern half of Tunisia. This portion of the country receives less than 7 inches of annual rainfall and, except for a few oases producing date palms, has virtually no agricultural value. Beneath the Sahara, however, are substantial deposits of natural resources, including phosphates and oil. Contrary to the stereotypical image, most of the Tunisian Sahara is not composed of rolling sand dunes; rather it is characterized by rocky, uneven

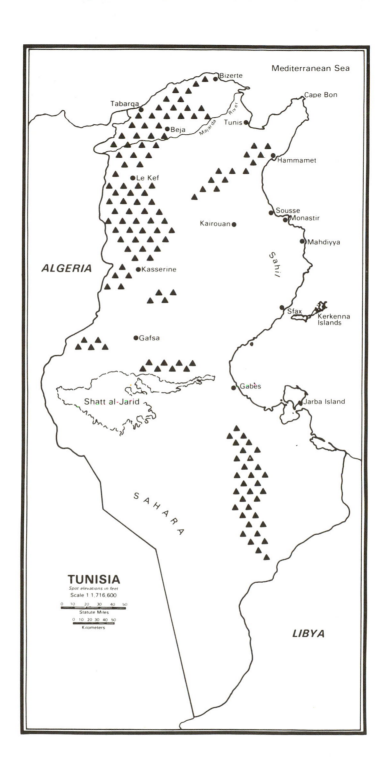

Mediterranean Sea

Cape Bon

Bizerte

Tabarqa

Majarda River

Tunis

Beja

ALGERIA

Le Kef

Hammamet

Kairouan

Sousse
Monastir

Mahdiyya

Kasserine

Sahil

Gafsa

Sfax
Kerkenna
Islands

Shatt al-Jarid

Gabes

Jarba Island

SAHARA

LIBYA

TUNISIA
Spot elevations in feet
Scale 1 1,716,600

0   10   20   30   40   50
Statute Miles

0   10   20   30   40   50
Kilometers

surfaces interspersed with several mountainous areas, the most notable of which are the Matmata chain and the Zahr to the south of Gabès.

An excellent network of roads and railways, many of them dating from the nineteenth century, ties Tunisia together and has helped to promote a sense of national identity. Several rail lines fanning out from Tunis serve the heavily populated northern quarter of the country, the only area in which the state-run system utilizes standard-gauge tracks. One route traverses the Majarda Valley and connects with the Algerian railway system west of Béja. A second joins Tunis with Tabarqa and includes a spur to the port of Bizerte. An important narrow-gauge line links the capital with the Sahil and runs roughly parallel to the east coast from Tunis to Gabès. Plans to convert this line to standard gauge and extend it to the Libyan frontier, thereby providing continuous standard-gauge track from Morocco to Libya, have been thwarted by recurrent political difficulties between Tunisia and Libya. Other narrow-gauge tracks, used almost exclusively for freight, branch off from this coastal line. They give access to the phosphate-producing areas in the west and south and also provide a rail link with the Jarid oasis of Tozeur.

Tunisia's relatively small size has made it feasible, in terms of both economy and efficiency, to move substantial amounts of freight and passengers on the country's 6,500 miles of paved roads. The Société Nationale des Transports operates trucking lines and manages some 150 bus routes providing passenger service to every portion of the country. An additional 3,800 miles of unpaved roads connect even remote villages with each other and with local market towns. Such roads, however, are often impassable after heavy rains or only negotiable by all-terrain vehicles, thus limiting their usefulness.

International trade is conducted through five seaports, of which Bizerte is the largest and most important. The next most active is Sfax, through which most of the country's crucial exports of olive oil and phosphates pass. The port of Tunis (actually located at La Goulette, a few miles from the capital) is smaller, as are the ports of Sousse and Gabès, although the last has been expanded and improved considerably in recent years. La Skirrah, between Sfax and Gabès, is Tunisia's only oil-exporting facility. A pipeline links La Skirrah with oil fields in the Algerian Sahara, enabling the port to load oil from that region as well as from the Tunisian south.

The Tunis-Carthage Airport, just outside the capital, is the main international airfield. The airports at Monastir (near Sousse) and Tozeur and on the island of Jarba are geared almost exclusively to tourist traffic. Sfax, Bizerte, and a number of smaller cities have regular air service provided by Tunis Air, the national carrier in which the government holds a controlling interest.

THE PEOPLE

Ethnic Groups

Most of Tunisia's more than 7 million people are Arabs, although a small Berber minority, estimated at no more than 2 percent of the total population, lives in the south, particularly on the island of Jarba. The terms *Arab* and *Berber* are best understood as linguistic rather than racial references, for modern Tunisians are an amalgamation of many ethnic groups, with the Arabs having made their appearance no earlier than the seventh century A.D. The words *Arabophone* and *Berberophone*, though clumsy, are more accurate descriptions.

Although scholars have long debated the origins of the Berbers, they have failed to formulate a universally accepted theory. In southern Tunisia, archeologists have discovered evidence of a Neolithic culture they have named Capsian (from Capsa, the ancient site near which the city of Gafsa now stands) dating from the tenth millennium B.C. During succeeding ages, migratory waves from the south and the east, and possibly from the north, resulted in the formation of a group of people whom the ancient Greeks called *barbaroi* (barbarians) because their customs varied so greatly from the behavior Hellenic civilization deemed proper. Our word *Berber* is derived from this derogatory term. These "indigenous" North African peoples managed to retain their identity in the face of subsequent Phoenician and Roman occupations of their land, although some of the Berbers, who were pagans, did convert to Judaism and later to Christianity. The Arab invasions of the seventh century initiated a much more widespread process of conversion to Islam, along with a tendency toward Arabization. This assimilation to the manners and language of the Arab conquerors proceeded slowly, however, and resulted in an Arabic-speaking majority only in the modern era.

Arabs and Berbers are not the sole ancestors of today's Tunisians. During the Christian Reconquest of Spain, many Muslims from Andalusia sought refuge in Tunisia and, in time, merged with the existing population. Later, in the centuries when the Ottoman Empire ruled Tunisia and much of the rest of North Africa, Turks and other Levantines contributed to the population mixture, although their impact was largely confined to the major urban centers. Sub-Saharan blacks, many of whom entered Tunisia as slaves, constitute yet another strand in the population. Some southern Europeans, especially Sicilians and

Maltese, migrated to Tunisia and became assimilated, adding another Mediterranean element to the heritage of contemporary Tunisia.

Unlike the native Tunisian Christians, who died out centuries ago, a community of Tunisian Jews remains, which traces its roots to the early years of the Diaspora. Estimated at some 58,000 when Tunisia became independent in 1956, this community diminished to fewer than 15,000 in the 1980s. Many Jews, uncertain of the attitude of the new government toward religious minorities, left in 1956. Attacks on synagogues during the 1967 Arab-Israeli War precipitated another wave of Jewish departures. Today, a small Jewish community still lives on the island of Jarba, but more than 80 percent of the present Jewish inhabitants reside in the capital, Tunis.

Urban-Rural Divisions

Slightly more than one-half of all Tunisians now live in cities and towns with populations in excess of 2,000. Most of the remainder are sedentary cultivators. Nomadism based on camel or sheep herding, once common in the steppes and the desert, has dwindled to almost the vanishing point. The urban population is increasing at a rate of 4 percent a year (in comparison with a national rate of roughly 2.5 percent annually and a rate in rural areas of barely 1 percent a year). These figures reveal the rapid growth of cities and towns at the expense of the countryside, whose inhabitants are moving in large numbers to the cities in search of better opportunities. What the figures do not reveal—at least not without a glance at a map—is that, because most major urban centers are in either the northeast or the Sahil, this internal migration has resulted in an emphasis on those regions and the location of many development projects in them. The country's interior, which has fewer cities to act as magnets, has, until very recently, received much less attention and, consequently, far fewer economic benefits. The people of the interior, resentful of the disproportionate attention paid to the country's Mediterranean fringe, have been the main participants in the exodus to the coast.

The development of Tunis has been particularly striking. With over 1 million residents and a population that continues to mushroom at the rate of about 5 percent a year, the capital houses almost one-third of the nation's urban dwellers and one-sixth of its total inhabitants. Nevertheless, the city's share of the nation's total urban population has decreased since independence because of the simultaneous expansion of Sfax, Sousse, Bizerte, Kairouan, and smaller cities, but it is still twice the size of the next largest city, Sfax. The traditional role of Tunis as the cultural and political heart of the country, however, assures it pride of place on the urban scene.

Livelihoods

The country's economically active population is divided almost equally among the agricultural, industrial, and service sectors. Almost a third of all cultivable land is used for growing cereals, particularly hard wheat (which produces the semolina used in making couscous, the national dish), barley, oats, and sorghum. As a general rule, however, the cereal harvest does not meet the internal demand, and some cereals must be imported. Olives are the next most significant crop, and Tunisia ranks high among the world's exporters of olive oil. Once confined largely to the Sahil, olive cultivation has recently been expanded into other parts of the country. Citrus fruits, grapes, vegetables grown on an increasing number of truck farms, and dates from the Saharan oases round out Tunisia's crops. Despite the spread of agricultural mechanization, labor-intensive procedures remain the norm on at least half of the land under cultivation, particularly on the smaller holdings in less fertile parts of the country.

Although forests cover only a small portion of Tunisia's land, some commercial cork production takes place in the northwest. The fishing grounds off Tunisia's coast constitute a potentially bountiful resource that has never been fully exploited. Relatively few Tunisians, most of them from cities and villages in the Sahil, earn their livelihood primarily from the sea.

Like many developing countries, Tunisia has stressed industrialization, frequently under state direction, as a means of enhancing self-sufficiency and earning revenue through exports. The greatest success in the export category has occurred in the petroleum and mineral industries. Although crude oil production is modest when compared with that of the Arabian peninsula states, or even with neighboring Algeria and Libya, Tunisian fields provide some 5 million tons of light-density oil per year for export. Unfortunately, this type of oil is not suitable for most of the country's domestic needs, and Tunisia must continue to import significant quantities of heavy-density crude. Phosphates are Tunisia's next most important mineral resource. The government has attempted to compensate for the decline in world demand for this mineral by minimizing the country's reliance on the export of raw phosphates. Instead, the government has built factories, especially fertilizer plants, to process the raw material into products that have a greater international demand.

The textile industry has also secured important overseas markets, but competition from European manufacturers benefiting from protectionist tariffs has hurt Tunisian entrepreneurs and diminished export earnings in recent years. Government efforts to encourge foreign

Date palms in a Saharan oasis. (Photo courtesy of Lewis B. Ware)

investment in the 1970s have led to the establishment of textile plants, and other factories as well, that are little more than assembly lines for goods whose components are granted duty-free entry to the country on condition that the finished product be exported. This arrangement allows foreign investors to take advantage of the significant cost differential between Tunisian and European labor. Advocates of such "offshore" industries assert that they broaden the government's tax base, although taxes are frequently forgiven or deferred for a specified period as an attraction to investors. Proponents also argue that the industries generate much needed employment for Tunisians, although generally only at low wages, and that they provide workers with technical or managerial skills, although often for only a small percentage of the Tunisians they employ. In final analysis, their contribution to the industrialization and economic development of the country is at best debatable.

A state-managed textile company, along with smaller, privately owned factories, serves internal needs, but the largest industry primarily focused on the home market is food processing. Even in this area, however, some commodities (olive oil, tuna fish) have long been exported, and government and private business efforts are continuing to discover new markets for these and other Tunisian foodstuffs. The construction industry is necessarily at the heart of all industrialization programs, and modern steel and cement factories sprang up in the years after independence. These factories meet only part of the nation's demand for material needed for new factories, housing units, and public works projects.

Another major Tunisian industry—second only to petroleum in earnings—is tourism. Tunisia has turned its Mediterranean beaches and desert oases into popular European vacation resorts. Because of the rush to construct new hotels and otherwise profit from the tourist boom, some prime agricultural land has been removed from production without providing sufficient alternative employment for those displaced. The service nature of tourism has created unique problems in this formerly colonized society, particularly since so many tourists are nationals of the former colonizing power. Finally, tourism is an industry over which Tunisians can exert only limited control because it is contingent on a great many factors (weather and the state of the visitors' economy, for example) that they are powerless to influence.

Art, Music, and Literature

Art. Over the centuries, Tunisian artists, musicians, and artisans have displayed great vitality in their cultural pursuits. As with so many aspects of modern Tunisian life, the country's fine arts bear the imprint of both its Arabo-Islamic and European heritages. Portraits, landscapes, and other types of painting intended to be displayed publicly or to adorn the home of a private purchaser hardly existed in Tunisia until the last century. Nor did sculpture. These limitations resulted from the belief held in the rigidly monotheistic early Muslim community that Christian religious paintings (especially Byzantine icons) and statuary constituted objects of worship. To avoid a similar situation in Islam and to preclude the possibility of an artist's depiction of living figures being even roughly equated with the divine act of creation, such art forms were discouraged in any religious context.

Although not absolutely forbidding figural representations, this attitude did impose limits on their use. Its result was to restrict painting largely to the illustration of manuscripts, with the miniature painting becoming perhaps the most highly refined Islamic art form. Lacking an alternative outlet, sculpture fared less well than painting and played virtually no role in classical Muslim society. Not until the nineteenth and twentieth centuries, during which Muslims experienced prolonged and intensive exposure to Western artistic and cultural values, did painters begin to probe beyond the traditional limitations on their art and a few practitioners of the plastic arts appear.

In Tunisia, as elsewhere, much of the work of these early artists was slavishly imitative of the newly discovered Western models. In time, however, they developed and perfected techniques of their own, which often combined modern theories and approaches with traditional forms such as the miniature. Much modern Tunisian art reflects broad national concerns, celebrating patriotic Tunisian themes or capturing aspects of a rapidly fading traditional society. The government has patronized the arts by encouraging the inclusion of indigenous art works in public buildings. The Union Nationale des Arts Plastiques et Graphiques provides an additional stimulus to the arts. In 1977 a museum of modern art, the Centre d'Art Vivant de la Ville de Tunis, opened in the capital.

Handicrafts made by highly trained and specialized artisans offered another outlet for artistic expression in the classical Muslim period and, to a certain extent, continue to do so. Tunisian artisans produce pottery, metalwork, and leather goods displaying traditional designs, whereas weavers create carpets embellished with a wide variety of complex geometric patterns. Demand for many craft items by tourists in Tunisia has risen more rapidly than traditional production methods can accommodate. In some instances, this market has led to the mass production of goods previously manufactured in limited quantities by hand; in the process traditional workers are often displaced, and the quality of the product is sacrificed.

Music. Traditional Tunisian music bears unmistakable signs of Iberian influences. Songs introduced into the country by refugees from Spain in the fifteenth and sixteenth centuries quickly formed the core of Tunisian popular music. Performed in local dialects rather than in classical Arabic, they are called *maluf.* In the contemporary period, Western tastes have affected music, just as they have art. Widespread radio ownership, or at least availability, coupled with the ease with which broadcasts from southern Europe may be heard in Tunisia, has created a taste for Western popular music, particularly among young persons. Even during the protectorate years, European music gained a small audience among westernized Tunisians.

Many traditional instruments began to give way to similar modern ones of European origin, thus threatening Tunisia's musical heritage. To forestall such a prospect, a national conservatory, dedicated to the preservation of classical Tunisian genres, was established in 1935. Since independence, the government has encouraged extensive efforts by the national orchestra to record traditional music. The entertainment presented at tourist centers often incorporates traditional music and dance but in bastardized forms calculated to appeal to visitors' preconceived stereotypes of Arabo-Islamic culture. In contrast, an annual festival at Testur celebrates the maluf in their unadulterated form and has contributed to keeping the traditional alive.

Literature. Many intellectuals who lived in what became Tunisia profoundly influenced pre-modern Arabo-Islamic culture. Since these men wrote exclusively in Arabic, however, the works of only the few who have attracted the interest of translators are familiar in the West. Perhaps the best known author is Ibn Khaldun, a fourteenth-century intellectual whose career began in the Hafsid court but who eventually held important political appointments in both North Africa and the Middle East. His best known work is the *Muqaddima (Introduction).* Drawing on his own experiences and observations, Ibn Khaldun wrote the *Muqaddima* in 1377 as the prelude to a universal history. It presents a detailed philosophy of history and explores at length the evolution of human societies; it became available to European readers only in the 1860s.

Imam Sahnun, an eighth-century religious scholar, was the author of *al-Mudawwana (The Collected Writings),* an early and extremely important source of Maliki law. More than any other individual, he was responsible for implanting and spreading the Maliki *madhhab* (a school of legal interpretation deriving its name from Malik ibn Anas, its founder) throughout the Maghrib. Ibn Rashiq, though not of North

African origin, spent much of his life in eleventh-century Kairouan. His poetry and his essays on literary criticism were widely hailed throughout the Arabic-speaking world of his day.

In the nineteenth and twentieth centuries, language itself became an issue for intellectuals. As the use of French spread among educated Tunisians, more and more writers adopted that language as the medium for their work. In so doing, however, they cut themselves off from much of their potential Tunisian audience. Similarly, the ideals and aspirations of those writers and poets who continued to use Arabic exclusively were inaccessible to the Europeans who exercised political and economic power in the protectorate. Although the Neo-Dustur leadership was heavily French speaking, many Tunisian writers in the inter-war period utilized their native tongue to emphasize Tunisia's Arabo-Islamic identity. Prominent among these men were the poet Abu al-Qasim Shabbi (1909–1934) and the writer Tahar Haddad (1899–1935). Each man's works, in Arabic, focused on themes of national pride and identity. Haddad published a particularly controversial book advocating reforms designed to achieve greater female emancipation and a more significant role for women in Tunisian society.

Drama and the novel were not genres customarily employed by classical Muslim men of letters, but they were introduced to the Middle East and North Africa with the coming of European colonialism. As a result, they did not blossom until the late nineteenth and early twentieth centuries and were, at first, the almost exclusive domain of authors trained in westernized schools. Poetry, a much more common literary vehicle in traditional Arab societies, had a natural appeal even to the Western educated, many of whom produced extensive bodies of poetry in European languages.

Tunisia's most widely acclaimed novelist writing in French is Albert Memmi. As a Jew growing up under the protectorate, Memmi was doubly aware of the problems faced by individuals pressed into positions of subordination. In the late 1950s, he left Tunisia for a self-imposed exile in France. Many of his works exploring themes of deracination and the difficulties of meaningful cross-cultural contacts have been translated into English. They include *The Pillar of Salt* (first published in 1953) and *The Scorpion* (1969). *The Colonizer and the Colonized*, an extremely powerful essay analyzing the relationship between these two groups from the perspective of the colonized is probably Memmi's best known work. A second highly respected Tunisian novelist utilizing French is Hashmi Bakush. His autobiographical novel *Ma foi demeure* (1958) explores questions similar to those raised by Memmi but from the viewpoint of a Tunisian Muslim.

Bakush is also the author of a historical novel, *La Dame de Carthage*, written in 1961. Well-known poets writing in French include Munsif-Tayyib Brahim, Ahmad Hamuda, and Ridha Zili.

The body of literature in Arabic has grown greatly since independence, but few of its authors are known in the West. Among the best established Tunisian novelists regularly using the language are Ali al-Duaji, Rashid al-Hamzawi, Bashir Khrayyif, and Mustafa Tlili.

Izz al-Din al-Madani has been a major contributor to the growth of Arabic theatre in Tunisia, as was Ali Ben Ayad, the country's best known dramatist and director at the time of his premature death in the early 1970s. Ben Ayad devoted considerable effort to staging theatrical performances outside the major urban centers to which they were usually restricted. His work as an actor and director brought him recognition not only in Tunisia and the Arab world, but also in France, where he staged several highly acclaimed productions in the late 1960s.

2

Pre-Islamic Tunisia

CARTHAGE

The appearance of Phoenician merchants in the central and western Mediterranean around the first millennium B.C. brought about profound changes. The Phoenicians dotted both sides of the sea with a chain of colonies designed to facilitate commerce by serving as both trading posts and stopover points for their vessels. One such colony, traditionally said to have been founded by settlers from Tyre in 814 B.C., was called Qart Hadasht (Carthage), meaning "new city." Its location on the Gulf of Tunis near the center of the Phoenician trading sphere assured its prosperity, and by the sixth century B.C. the Carthaginians were taking advantage of their central location to develop a commercial empire of their own. The continuing infusion of new immigrants from Tyre swelled the city's population and fostered a respect for the traditions of their home country.

Because the Carthaginians imported their religion, their laws, and their governmental concepts from the more sophisticated lands of the Near East, they exposed the indigenous Berbers to a more complex and fully developed culture. This exposure set in motion the integration of the Berbers into a Mediterranean world in which they had previously functioned only on the fringes. The dichotomy between the lifestyle of the urban (and urbane) Carthaginians and that of the primitive, rural-dwelling Berbers was immediately apparent. Aside from commercial transactions, limited contact occurred between the two groups, and each retained a clear sense of identity.

Greek merchants offering higher quality goods than the Carthaginians began to penetrate many of their rivals' traditional preserves in the sixth and fifth centuries B.C. They threatened to devastate Carthage's commerce by restricting it to the least developed and, therefore, least profitable areas of the central and western Mediterranean. The Carthaginians, who had little enthusiasm for warfare, recruited Berber mercenaries for a campaign to secure western Sicily,

15

in the belief that control of that part of the island would block further
Greek advances. At the same time, they allied themselves with the
Etruscans, who also feared Greek ascendancy and with whom the
Carthaginians were prepared to share western Mediterranean markets.
Greek forces defeated the Carthaginians on Sicily at the Battle of
Himera in 480 B.C., but the victors' failure to conquer all the island
enabled Carthage to retain its commercial importance.

A second round of economic warfare with the Greeks, in which
the Carthaginian strategy again centered on holding at least western
Sicily, erupted toward the end of the fifth century B.C. The Carthaginian
mercenaries fared better in battle than they had at Himera, but the
oligarchy ruling the city was reluctant to commit its resources to a
sustained military struggle. Moreover, the wealthy businessmen worried that the mercenaries might acquire too much power and assert
themselves on the domestic political scene to their own detriment.
The Carthaginian hesitancy to plunge into an extended conflict allowed
the Greeks to ignore a peace agreement calling for the division of
Sicily, and Dionysius, the tyrant of Syracuse, continued to champion
the Greek cause against Carthage on the island. After several decades
of indecisive fighting and negotiating, Dionysius agreed to a division
of Sicily around 360 B.C.; he did so less out of fear of Carthage than
out of desire to free himself to meet the more serious challenge posed
by the increasingly powerful Italian cities. But even this arrangement
did not end Greco-Carthaginian confrontations. In less than half a
century, a Greek army drawn from Cyrene (a Greek dependency in
what is now eastern Libya) and Syracuse invaded Africa and defeated
the Carthaginians on their own territory. Only the squabbles of the
victors prevented them from capitalizing on their success, and for a
second time Carthage emerged from hostilities with the Greeks with
most of its influence and power intact.

The wars were not without their effect, however. Despite the
enmity between the two sides, the prolonged contact of Carthage
with the rich culture of the Greek world resulted in an infusion of
Hellenistic influences, particularly in government and religion. The
more or less simultaneous demise of Tyre as a viable political entity
and the confirmation of Carthage as an important independent factor
in the Mediterranean, influenced by the civilizations around it but
with an identity of its own, hastened this process. There were other
changes as well. The wars' disruption of trade compelled Carthage
to devote more attention to agriculture. The city extended its control
further into the hinterland but made no effort to incorporate the
indigenous people more fully into its life. Despite occasional opportunities, the Carthaginians did not attempt to acquire many overseas

territories, contenting themselves with trading posts in coastal enclaves, and Carthage's small population precluded it from extensive colonization abroad. However, the city's failure to expand its human and material resource bases hurt its chances for survival when it came into conflict with Rome.

Although Rome initially cooperated with Carthage to curb the Greeks on Sicily, each suspected the other's motives as Greek power on that strategic island waned. From the Carthaginian perspective, the First Punic War (263 B.C.–241 B.C.) simply continued earlier engagements with the Greeks. After a few desultory Roman attacks in Sicily, the arena of combat switched to the sea. Carthage had a larger fleet than Rome and also enjoyed the theoretical advantage of greater naval experience, but Rome's superior technology made its warships more effective. Berber revolts during the war hampered Carthage and in 249 B.C. even prevented it from benefiting from the destruction of the Roman fleet at the siege of Lilybaeum. The Carthaginians adopted a cautious, defensive strategy that allowed Rome to rebuild its fleet, again seize the initiative, and inflict a crippling blow on the Carthaginian navy within less than a decade. Carthage had no choice but to abandon Sicily and sue for peace. The First Punic War neither brought down the curtain on Carthage as a Mediterranean power nor ended its rivalry with Rome. It was, instead, merely the opening act in a drama that continued for another century.

Hopes for a lasting peace dimmed as Rome threw down the gauntlet to Carthage by moving into the western Mediterranean, including the Iberian peninsula, long one of Carthage's most important markets. The inadequacy of their fleet in the First Punic War prompted the leaders of Carthage to devise a totally different strategy for the Second (218 B.C.–202 B.C.). Hannibal, a leading citizen, led the army in an overland attack against Italy from Carthaginian positions in Iberia. His troops' remarkable journey across the Alps gave them the advantage of surprise, but the vast resources and readily accessible reinforcements at the disposal of the Romans kept a decisive victory out of the invaders' grasp. Conversely, by severing Hannibal's links with his Iberian bases and by maintaining control of the sea lanes, Rome made it impossible to reinforce the Carthaginian army. With most of Carthage's army tied down in Italy, the Roman general Scipio successfully attacked Carthage itself, accepting its surrender in 203 B.C. Hannibal returned to Africa, but his exhausted army was defeated in the following year at the Battle of Zama in northwestern Tunisia.

After this second round of fighting, Rome imposed more stringent terms, forcing Carthage into an alliance subordinating it to Rome. To further constrain Carthage, the Romans rewarded the Berber chief

Masinissa, and others who had allied with them, with large grants of land around Carthage and the status of Roman clients. To ensure the effectiveness of this policy, Rome forbade Carthage to wage war without its consent. Though still not totally incapacitated, Carthage was crippled, and the ascendancy of the northern shores of the Mediterranean over the southern had begun to take shape.

Over the next several decades, Masinissa led the Berber tribes into a loose confederation. Despite Carthage's record of contempt toward his people, Masinissa admired its culture and promoted the incorporation of many of its features into Berber society. But the Carthaginians saw Masinissa as an obstacle to a restoration of their power, particularly in view of his links with Rome. When efforts to draw him into an anti-Roman alliance failed, Carthage's leaders began to lay plans for military action, but Rome intervened. In this Third Punic War (146 B.C.) Rome again invaded Carthage, this time destroying the city. Roman resolve to obliterate Carthage entirely, symbolized by the sowing of salt in its ruins, revealed the exhaustion of Rome's patience, but it was also an acknowledgment of how strong a force Carthage had once been and how much Rome continued to fear its old enemy, even as its own might grew. Many Carthaginians fled into the hinterland, taking with them traditions that had already begun to permeate the tribes and laying the groundwork for the mixed Berber-Carthaginian culture that soon would characterize rural North Africa.

The centuries of Carthaginian control made what is modern Tunisia an active and permanent participant in the Mediterranean cultural complex because Carthage's commercial ventures exposed it to all the other dynamic civilizations of the Mediterranean basin. As a colony of the Phoenicians and a competitor of Greece and Rome, Carthage introduced new ideas and values into the area. Despite the Carthaginians' inclination to keep the indigenous society at arm's length, their presence could not fail to influence the Berbers. The inability of Carthage to match the far greater human and material resources of Rome or its rival's more highly developed political culture ultimately led to Roman supremacy. Nevertheless, the most important legacy of Carthage—having made its domain a focal point of Mediterranean society—endured. The land that had been Carthage was never again merely at the periphery of Mediterranean civilization; it continued to fulfill the function first given it by Carthage—to serve as a meeting point for ideas and peoples from the eastern Mediterranean and its northern shores.

ROMAN RULE

A Roman *praetor* oversaw the former Carthaginian territory, now designated as the province of Africa. He resided at Utica, a city previously allied to Carthage and some 20 miles northwest of it. Masinissa died soon after the destruction of Carthage. The Romans allowed his sons to divide his territories, but at the same time they tightened their grip on Numidia (as they called the Berber-controlled land of what is now eastern Algeria) by establishing a protectorate there.

Some wealthy Romans acquired Carthaginian land, much of which had entered the public domain, and began developing large estates (*latifundia*) using Berber and Punic laborers, but Rome undertook no official colonization projects until around 105 B.C. At that time, Roman soldiers, who had foiled the attempt by Jugurtha, Masinissa's grandson, to reunify his ancestral domain, received small land grants in Africa and Numidia. More numerous grants to veterans of the civil wars that later destroyed the Republic, including one by Julius Caesar to members of an expedition that deposed Juba, a Numidian king who had sided with Pompey, further Romanized the territory.

To facilitate its domination, the empire annexed portions of Numidia and, in 27 B.C., joined them to the old Carthaginian lands to form a new province, Africa Proconsularis. Caesar also ordered the reconstruction of Carthage, and some descendants of the Punic population returned to the city. Within two centuries, it had become the third most important community in the empire, behind only Alexandria and Rome itself.

Those centuries coincided with the dramatic growth and prosperity of the province. Its agricultural potential and the accessibility of the Roman market attracted migrants driven from the Italian peninsula by political and demographic pressures. As many new towns took root in the Majarda Valley and along the coast, agriculture replaced commerce as the mainstay of the economy. Africa's farmland produced olives and grapes, but wheat was by far the most important crop. Africa Proconsularis exported two-thirds of its cereal production, earning the province the title "Granary of Rome."

To prevent nomadic incursions into the sown lands, a network of forts and physical barriers was erected along the province's western and southern frontiers. Within Africa Proconsularis itself, Roman administrators confined some nomads to reservations under military control, whereas others lost access to their traditional pastures as the

Roman ruins at Thuburbo Majus. (Photo courtesy of Lewis B. Ware)

new municipalities absorbed their grazing land for farming. Although animosity had marked the relations between nomadic and sedentary populations in the Carthaginian era, Rome's greater power to jeopardize the nomads heightened the tensions. Those tribespeople who attempted, or were forced, to adjust to the new agricultural economy found only marginal parcels of land available, and many were reduced to tenancy on large estates owned by absentee landlords.

The distinctions between the owners of the land and those who worked it confined the process of romanization to the growing number of cities and towns. In them, Roman colonists married into the more successful and ambitious indigenous families, gradually forming an influential aristocracy. Only a few Africans chose to assimilate Roman culture, however, and a socioeconomic hierarchy of Romans, Romanized Africans, and unassimilated Africans never disappeared. The use of the Latin language spread, but it did not supplant either the Berber or Punic dialects. Nor did the Roman imperial cults that naturally appeared among the settlers displace Berber and Punic rituals, although many of the latter adapted and incorporated Roman practices. In the words of one scholar of the period, "the Romans . . . gave [Africa] peace and made her prosperous, but they never made her Roman."[1]

Africa's prosperity proved a mixed blessing. Burdened by heavy taxes imposed from Rome, its cities revolted in A.D. 238, proclaiming Gordianus, the provincial governor, as emperor. The imperial authorities called upon the Numidian Legion, a unit composed largely of Berber conscripts and responsible for policing Numidia, which had become a separate military governorate in the previous century, to crush the revolt. In its enthusiasm, the legion sacked the major cities of Africa Proconsularis. Few ever fully recovered, and the province's economic center of gravity shifted more firmly than ever to the smaller villages of the interior where the revolt had been less disruptive. Urban decline resulted in higher rural taxes, ruining most of the peasant cultivators who had managed to retain their land. Anger among rural inhabitants, easily translatable into hostility between Berbers and the Roman or romanized population, grew and engendered an air of instability throughout much of the third century. The extension of Christianity during the same period provided a vehicle for the expression of local antagonisms.

Evidence of Christian communities in Africa Proconsularis dates from about 180; by 200 Carthage had become the seat of a bishop. Conversions to the new faith first occurred in the cities, but the mounting rural discontent of the mid-third century left many Berbers receptive to religious precepts directly challenging the Roman gods

and, through them, the imperial administration. Many converted, often more as an expression of anti-Roman sentiment than from any sincere acceptance of Christian theology.

Just as adhesion to Christianity often expressed general uneasiness rather than specifically religious dissatisfaction, a fourth-century schism within the African Church reflected social and economic ills as much as sacred concerns. Christians, who had clung tenaciously to their faith during the empirewide persecutions of Diocletian in 303 and who had seen many of their leaders martyred, looked upon churchmen who had not tried to resist the political authorities with suspicion and resentment. When one of these "yielders," Caecilian, became bishop of Carthage a decade later, a council of bishops led by Donatus condemned him. The Donatists claimed that Caecilian's expedient behavior had placed him outside the church and that he could no longer administer the sacraments. The Roman and Romanized population of the cities of Africa Proconsularis supported Caecilian, but the rural Berber Christians and their clerics, joined by the lower classes of Carthage, rallied behind the Donatist position. The latter group was composed of precisely the people who had suffered most in the recent economic upheavals. In accepting Donatism they not only made a religious statement but also challenged the "haves" of the society whom they blamed for the economic condition of the countryside. For the next century, Donatism and rural revolts went hand in hand. In the end, however, an external force—the Vandals—delivered the blow that broke the power of the Roman Empire in Africa.

The incorporation of modern Tunisia into the Roman sphere reinforced linkages to the Mediterranean world that had begun to form in the Carthaginian era. Under Rome's aegis, people and ideas from Mediterranean Europe, often the source of forces that would shape critical developments in later Tunisian history, exerted great influence for the first time. With the Roman occupation came a more intensive level of agricultural development and foreign settlement. As Roman interests threatened to relegate many Berbers to a marginal position, tensions between the nomadic and sedentary populations increased, finding expression in a variety of ways, including religion. Few of the rural Africans who converted to Christianity ever completely abandoned pre-Roman traditions and practices. In the towns and cities, however, romanization was more successful, creating an upper class associated with the conquerors and sharing many of their interests. The Donatist schism gave the Christian peasantry an opportunity to distinguish itself from an urban-based socioeconomic class with which it had little in common, including interpretations

of their shared religion. The potential for such a dual society had existed during Carthaginian times, but the more aggressive character of Rome, coupled with the presence of an effective mechanism for protest in Christianity, made the dualism both more apparent and more dangerous.

THE VANDALS

The pressure of barbarian tribes on Rome's European frontiers further diminished the already weakened imperial capacity to control Africa. The Vandals, a Germanic tribe from Spain, crossed the Mediterranean and reached Africa Proconsularis in 429, quickly mastering the entire province except for Carthage. The turmoil created by the revolt of Rome's military governor, Boniface, had prompted the Vandals to time their expedition as they did, but the need for additional sources of food had given the sharpest prod to their leader, Gunderic.

The Roman Empire initially hoped to treat the Vandals as federated allies—a practice it had adopted with many barbarian tribes in Europe. But when Gaiseric, Gunderic's successor, captured Carthage in 439 and began to mount raids against Sicily and Sardinia (culminating in the sack of Rome itself in 455), it had little choice but to acknowledge his sovereignty in Africa Proconsularis and Byzacenia, a recently created province encompassing the Sahil and southern Tunisia. For almost a century, the Vandals successfully resisted attempts to restore Roman control, repelling invading forces dispatched from Constantinople, the new imperial capital.

The Vandal kings ruled with a strong hand but left many existing institutions intact. They altered Roman laws and customs only minimally, and Romans continued to serve in the administration. The Vandal aristocracy did confiscate large rural estates but usually retained the former Roman owners as managers. Such moderation ensured that the Vandals' presence would not damage the very agricultural capacity that had originally attracted them to Africa. Indeed, after long years of disorder, the Vandals inaugurated an era of prosperity and tranquillity enabling them to solidify their hold over the area.

On the negative side, the Vandals segregated themselves from their subjects and emphasized their status as an alien ruling elite. They paid no taxes, shunned intermarriage with the local inhabitants, and, by relying on Berbers to fill the ranks of the army, abandoned their warrior traditions in favor of the luxuries of Roman civilization. The strongest factor setting the Vandals apart, however, was their steadfast belief in Arianism. This heretical doctrine represented for them not only a religious conviction but also a mark of distinction in a world dominated by Roman culture. The Vandals' zeal for Arianism led them to persecute Africa's other Christians. The latter turned to the emperor in Constantinople, Christianity's most powerful ruler, for help, but his own Orthodox beliefs left him unwilling to aid the Vandals' Catholic subjects. The Vandal king, Hilderic, took advantage of this turn of events to improve relations with the empire, forging an alliance that enabled him to focus his undivided attention on a problem more threatening than religious dissidence—that posed by hostile Berber tribes on the fringes of his kingdom.

To discourage urban revolts, the Vandals had permitted city defenses to fall into disrepair. Furthermore, their lack of interest in military matters resulted in the neglect of the defensive system designed by the Romans to hold the least manageable Berber tribes at bay. The danger of some tribes breaching these defenses and bursting into the plains, where they might wreak havoc on the settled economy, increased steadily through the early 500s. Hilderic's main attempt to meet this challenge failed when Berber tribespeople badly defeated his army in 530. This setback convinced the Vandal aristocracy, already disturbed by the king's alliance with the Byzantine Empire, of the need to depose Hilderic. His removal triggered a Byzantine intervention that ended the Vandal era.

Like the Roman period before it, the Vandal period illustrated the impact that the northern Mediterranean now had on Africa. The Vandals' initial aggressiveness allowed them to impose a much needed period of stability on the area, but they lacked the cultural baggage to devise the mechanisms of a permanent, viable state; they were unwilling to work within the framework of local interests even to the limited extent that the Romans had; and, as their military strength deteriorated, they could not, without popular support, resist the empire's efforts to reassert itself in Africa.

BYZANTINE AFRICA

Even before the Vandal state had begun to unravel, the rulers of Constantinople had contemplated an attack on Africa as part of a broader plan to bring areas once held by Rome under their administration. Hilderic's overthrow provided his Byzantine allies with a convenient pretext for an invasion. The Emperor Justinian's opposition to Arianism and the appeals of Roman citizens, fearful that continuing Vandal rule would ruin the province, made an expedition inevitable. In 533, Byzantine troops commanded by Belisarius landed south of Carthage and quickly overcame minimal Vandal resistance.

The Byzantines eliminated the Vandals as a factor in Africa as rapidly as they had become one in the previous century. Africa Proconsularis and Byzacenia formed the basis for a new Byzantine prefecture. Its government enslaved captured Vandal soldiers, excluded civilians from political office, encouraged its own troops to marry Vandal women, and seized Vandal lands. To the distress of the Byzantine warriors who wanted this property for themselves, much of it reverted to its previous Roman owners. Belisarius checked a mutiny of disgruntled soldiers in 536, but the eagerness of the Berber tribes to join that uprising foreshadowed serious troubles.

Byzantine attention to the economy, intended to revive the prosperity of earlier Roman times, invited increased Berber raids. Efforts to implant Byzantine influence throughout the reconquered provinces and encroachments into previously uncontrolled areas also provoked uprisings. The most serious, led by Antalas, the same chieftain who had defeated Hilderic, kept government forces out of most of Byzacenia from 544 to 548. Although the army eventually compelled Antalas and other Berber leaders to acknowledge grudgingly the reality of the Byzantine presence, it lacked both the will and the power to contain resistance by dismantling the tribal confederations. The Byzantines never felt safe from Berber attacks, leading them to adopt a defensive strategy that ultimately confined them to reinforceable positions along the coast and a handful of well-protected interior enclaves. This was simply the latest reflection of the pattern of rural Berber resentment of foreign mastery of the settled areas. The Byzantine authorities, unable to pacify the Berbers, did not believe they could accommodate African interests without compromising their own.

Religious controversies further destabilized Byzantine Africa. Its Christians refused to accept the Monophysite doctrine supported by Emperor Justinian at the time of the occupation. Their later rejection of the Monothelism favored by Emperor Heraclius triggered a rebellion in 638. Such theological differences weakened the province's links with Constantinople, and in 646 its governor, the exarch Gregory, declared his independence. These developments were occurring at the very time that the Arabs, inspired by their commitment to the Islamic faith, stood poised to sweep into a virtually defenseless Mediterranean Africa.

The Byzantine Empire failed to achieve its objectives in Africa. Debilitated by internal rebellions and external attacks, the emperors could not bring to bear sufficient resources to curb the Berber tribes, restore prosperity, or effectively incorporate the province into the imperial structure. The Byzantine era actually coincided with a diminution of Roman influences among the tribes. As happened in many other parts of the empire, dissent within the Christian community facilitated the advance of Islam that, in turn, precipitated major social changes. With the collapse of Gregory's resistance to the Muslims, centuries of Western influences, nurtured by Romans, Vandals, and the Byzantine heirs of Rome, drew to a close. As in Phoenician times, Semitic peoples from the eastern Mediterranean were to assert the dominant cultural influence on the peoples of what is now Tunisia.

NOTES

1. T.R.S. Broughton, *The Romanization of Africa Proconsularis* (Baltimore: Johns Hopkins, 1929), p. 228.

3

The Introduction of Islam and Arab Rule

THE ARAB CONQUEST, 647–800

An extraordinary burst of expansion carried the Arabs and their new faith, Islam, into Persia, Syria, and Egypt less than a decade after the death of the prophet Muhammad in 632. The Arabs knew little about the Maghrib—the land west of the Nile Valley—but the Caliph Uthman ordered raids into Byzantine Africa in 647, in part to belie his critics' charges that he had lost interest in enlarging the Muslim domain. Although his forces defeated Gregory at Sbaitla, they refrained from attacking any heavily defended Byzantine positions, as they were more attuned to guerrilla warfare and more confident in the desert and the steppes than on the coastal plain. Aware that their tactics left them vulnerable to counterattack from the Byzantine cities, the Arabs exacted an indemnity and withdrew in short order. The Byzantines' discomfort pleased the Berbers, who had closely observed the fighting but had pointedly not joined in. They chose instead to safeguard their independence by keeping their distance from the Arabs. Revolts in Egypt and Iraq during the final years of Uthman's reign, culminating in a five-year civil war after his death in 656, diverted Arab attention from North Africa.

The Umayyad Dynasty, emerging from this power struggle to preside over the Muslim community, renewed the African campaigns. Bedouin warriors led by Uqba ibn Nafi founded a garrison city, Kairouan, on the steppes some hundred miles southwest of Carthage in 670. This outpost served as the capital of the province of Ifriqiya (the Arabic form of the Latin *Africa*), a dependency of Egypt. The site of Kairouan again revealed the Arabs' preference for the hinterland and their intention of establishing a foothold there rather than on the coast—a policy that distinguished them from all the area's previous invaders. Both the Arabs and the Byzantines, who remained in their coastal enclaves, solicited Berber support, but the tribespeople saw no merit in aiding either contender. On the contrary, they organized a stiff resistance to the Arabs, whom they regarded as the more serious threat. The guerrilla attacks of Kusaila, the Berber leader, proved highly effective. In 683, one of his ambushes claimed the life of Uqba, and in the ensuing disorder he occupied Kairouan. The Arab response was slow because conditions in the Islamic heartlands were once again determining the pace of events in Ifriqiya. Until the last decade of the century, the Umayyads faced a variety of challenges to their rule. Only when they had successfully turned these aside could the caliphs concentrate on an area so remote from Damascus as Ifriqiya.

At the head of the most substantial Arab force yet to enter Africa, Hassan ibn Numan retook Kairouan in 691. Berber resistance continued, however, until the defeat in 698 of Kahina, a woman who had rallied the tribes in a final defensive effort. In the meantime, the Arabs had turned on the remaining Byzantine positions. Carthage fell in 695, but the Byzantine fleet recaptured it quickly. After again seizing Carthage in 698, the Arabs abandoned it, building a new city, Tunis, several miles inland. Situated on a lake connected to the sea by a narrow channel, Tunis enjoyed greater protection from naval attacks. Kairouan, however, remained the most important city of Ifriqiya, now a province in its own right, and the point of departure for expeditions into the rest of North Africa and the Iberian peninsula.

To promote Ifriqiya's incorporation into the Arabo-Islamic cultural sphere, the Umayyads encouraged Middle Eastern tribes to settle there, but the small number of Arabs who emigrated had a limited impact.[1] Although Arabic was the administrative language of the province, the rural Berbers constituting the bulk of the population made no effort to adopt it, as they had earlier shunned Latin. Islamization proceeded more rapidly, and many Berbers converted in order to join the advancing Muslim armies and reap some of the profits likely to accrue in campaigns elsewhere in the Maghrib and Spain. Conversion gave the Berbers limited access to the power enjoyed by the Arab ruling class without requiring the complete assimilation they had traditionally resisted. Most converts were pagans, for Islam recognized the Berber Christians and Jews as *ahl al-kitab*, or the recipients of a revealed religion who were entitled to the protection of the Islamic government and, upon payment of a small fee, to the right to practice their faith unhindered.

Rarely in the Umayyad Empire did non-Arab converts receive treatment equal to that afforded the Arabs. Descended from the mercantile oligarchy dominating Mecca in pre-Islamic times, the Umayyads reveled in their Arab identity and looked down on other peoples, even after they had accepted Islam. Their governors in Ifriqiya often imposed on Berber converts taxes prescribed only for non-Muslims, while limiting their military service to the least prestigious and least remunerative units. Various forms of social exclusion, including the discouragement of Berber-Arab marriages, generated deep resentment among the new adherents of Islam. Yet even in the best circumstances, Berber relations with the Umayyads would have proved troublesome. The attempt to control tribes that had avoided external interference for centuries naturally triggered antagonisms that the racist inclination of the ruling elite further aggravated.

This situation made the Berbers susceptible to Kharajism, a doctrine that asserted that any pious Muslim might be caliph and that by extension stood for the equality of all Muslims. Kharajite-inspired Berber rebellions in the 730s and 740s, mostly west of Ifriqiya where Umayyad control was most tenuous, revealed the virulent nature of the movement. At the same time and for many of the same reasons, a tide of anti-Umayyad sentiment swept through Persia. Descendants of the prophet Muhammad's uncle Abbas overthrew the dynasty in 750, raising support with promises of equality guaranteed by the leadership of the prophet's family.

Abbasid governors soon arrived in Ifriqiya, as did missionaries bent on counteracting Kharajite propaganda. Despite increased Arab-Berber contacts, many Berbers clung to Kharajism as an effective means of rallying opposition to outside control. Uprisings during the first thirty years of Abbasid rule gave Kharajite warriors control of Kairouan on several occasions. The province burdened the Baghdad caliphs more than it benefited them, which explains their relative lack of concern when it slipped from their grasp at the start of the ninth century.

As with previous conquerors, the Arabs more readily mastered those sedentary regions in which the survival of agriculture and commerce depended on the stability that only a strong central government could guarantee. The decline of Byzantine authority and the concomitant increase in Berber pressures on these areas immediately preceding the Arab invasion greatly facilitated the Arabs' acquisition of Ifriqiya. Their proclivity for the desert and the steppes intensified their contacts with the Berbers, making a working arrangement with the tribes both more imperative and more difficult than it had been for the Phoenicians, Romans, Vandals, or Byzantines. The prospect of enjoying at least some of the advantages of the ruling elite sparked the Berbers' initial interest in Islam, but the exclusivist policies of the Umayyads made their full integration into Arabo-Islamic society virtually impossible. Perhaps the feature most clearly distinguishing the early Muslim era from earlier periods of outside control in Ifriqiya was the decisive role played by conditions in the conquerors' homeland in determining the region's fate. The first concerns of Damascus and Baghdad were events in the Middle East. Those events often, if not always appropriately, set the tone for policies elsewhere, including in the Maghrib. By the same token, the timing of the imperial government's concentration on the more remote provinces depended on the presence or absence of problems closer to home. Both physical and psychic distance paved the way for the rise of viable autonomous rulers concerned primarily with Ifriqiya.

THE AGHLABID DYNASTY, 800–909

Late in the eighth century, the Abbasids called upon Ibrahim ibn Aghlab, their governor of the Mzab (a group of Saharan oases in what is now Algeria), to quell the disorders plaguing Ifriqiya. Ibrahim agreed, on condition that the caliph grant him and his heirs full civil and military power as autonomous *amir*s, a title implying independent authority. In return, Ibrahim promised to send an annual tribute to the caliph whom he acknowledged as *amir al-muminin* (commander of the faithful), or spiritual head of the Muslim community. The arrangement satisfied both parties: The caliph could no longer directly control Ifriqiya in any case, whereas Baghdad's bestowal of autonomy on Ibrahim greatly enhanced his stature. Not surprisingly, the Aghlabids looked to Baghdad for examples of proper military, governmental, and administrative behavior. The Abbasids viewed such nominal influence in Ifriqiya as preferable to no influence.

From the outset, however, the dynasty faced opposition from several sources. Its contemptuous treatment of the Berbers kept Arab-Berber relations tense as new problems arose among the Arab soldiers themselves. The Aghlabid army consisted primarily of tribespeople from the Middle East or their descendants. It reflected the factionalism that political upheavals in the Muslim heartlands had instilled among the tribes, compromising their ability to work together effectively. Consequently, the amirs recruited slave troops and mercenaries and also engineered overseas adventures to remove the army from Ifriqiya and minimize the possibility of its meddling in political activities.

Since the Arab conquest, Kairouan had become a religious center, disseminating Islamic thought to the rest of the Maghrib. The influential *ulama* (Muslim religious officials) of Kairouan objected to the Aghlabid practice of levying agricultural taxes not specifically sanctioned by

The village of Korbous on the Cape Bon peninsula. (Photo courtesy of Lewis B. Ware)

the Quran. But Aghlabid acceptance, in imitation of the Abbasids, of the Hanafite madhhab constituted a more fundamental irritant to the ulama who much preferred the concepts of the school founded by Malik ibn Anas (the Maliki madhhab). Although the rulers initially pressed their view, they eventually recognized the need to accede to the majority of their subjects' wishes in this sensitive matter. By the middle of the ninth century, the post of chief *qadi* (judge presiding over a court rendering decisions according to the *sharia*, or Islamic law) of Kairouan was a Maliki preserve. The entrenchment of the Maliki school provided the people of Ifriqiya with a clearly Muslim identity that also stressed their separation from the Middle East. Malikism remains to this day the madhhab of virtually all North African Muslims.

The conquest of Sicily in the middle of the ninth century marked the zenith of the Aghlabid era. Since Carthaginian times, the rulers of northern Africa had kept a wary eye on Sicily and the Muslims well knew the potential danger of its use as a base for Byzantine naval operations. The Aghlabid campaign against the island opened in the 820s, when Byzantine dissidents requested their assistance. Once ensconced on the island, the Aghlabids had no intention of withdrawing. By midcentury they controlled all of Sicily and were using it to launch attacks against the Italian mainland. The Aghlabids made a virtue of necessity, customarily portraying these expeditions as *jihad*s (struggles on behalf of Islam) and using them to stress the dynasty's commitment to the faith and its right to rule. In light of the religious differences with their subjects, charges of un-Islamic behavior by the ulama, and their political break with the East, the Aghlabids emphasized these expressions of legitimacy as strongly as possible.

At the same time, they took care not to allow the hostilities to jeopardize commerce. In addition to its religious role, the Aghlabids had developed Kairouan into an important entrepôt whose merchants shipped slaves and other sub-Saharan commodities to lucrative Middle Eastern markets. The dynasty also cultivated cross-Mediterranean trade, and although Aghlabid raiders preyed on shipping in Sicilian and Italian waters, they rarely molested vessels conducting business with Muslims. Some southern Italian communities even allied themselves with the Aghlabids. These examples of commerce transcending religious considerations provided ammunition for Aghlabid critics who unsuccessfully sought to topple the dynasty by challenging its religious fervor. On a more positive note, they brought substantial economic benefits to many in Ifriqiya, strengthening the links between rulers and ruled and giving the Aghlabids a measure of popular support unprecedented in their reign.

Revenues amassed through conquest and trade financed both rural improvements and urban growth. The amirs constructed extensive irrigation canals and reservoirs that increased agricultural productivity, thus helping to support the growing number of urban dwellers. To guarantee the security of the many towns and villages on the coast vulnerable to attack as long as the campaigns in Sicily and Italy continued, the Aghlabids built *ribat*s, or fortified mosques, at key points along the shoreline.

The reign of Ibrahim II (875–902) convincingly demonstrated that Ifriqiya's stability depended not only on the state guarding against threats from Europe but also on its capacity to maintain the support of the sedentary population. It had to adhere to sound, equitable economic policies and protect the settled population from nomadic incursions without driving the nomads into a coalition against the dynasty. Despite a series of climatic disasters and inadequate harvests during his reign, Ibrahim II insisted on levying excessive taxes, largely to finance the construction of Raqqada, his royal city just outside Kairouan. Even the amir's notable successes in Sicily failed to offset the antagonism his fiscal policies created among his subjects. To make matters worse, his overseas activities drew troops from Ifriqiya's western frontiers just as a serious threat was emerging there. Propagandists for Shii Islam (the religiopolitical movement that insisted that only descendants of Ali, the prophet Muhammad's cousin and son-in-law, were acceptable *imams*, or leaders, of the Muslim community) attempted to win support for their cause among the Muslim Berber tribes by sowing dissatisfaction with the Abbasid caliphate and, by extension, with its agents, the Aghlabids. The independent nature of the Berber tribespeople predisposed them to such appeals against authority, and the generally poor treatment that the Aghlabids had accorded their Berber coreligionists increased their susceptibility. For many of the same reasons that had led their ancestors to embrace Donatism, many now turned to Shii Islam.

The Aghlabid family realized that Ibrahim II could not master the Shii threat and that the continuation of his reign merely provided critics with a choice target. The caliphs, despite a century of abstaining from Ifriqiya's affairs, deemed the situation sufficiently critical to encourage the Aghlabid princes' demand for Ibrahim's abdication. His successor's opposition to the Maliki madhhab—which may have been intended to tighten the province's links with Baghdad—deprived him of local backing and resulted in his assassination a few months after taking over. The last Aghlabid, Ziyadat Allah III, gained power by murdering rivals among his relatives. In addition to weakening the family's solidarity, the actions of Ziyadat Allah lent credence to the accusations of immorality leveled at the Aghlabid amirs by the Shia from the start of their campaign.

As Aghlabid fortunes ebbed in the early tenth century, those of the Shia rose. Their principal agent, Abu Abdallah, summoned to North Africa Ubaidallah, a descendant of Ismail, the man whom the most militant Shia recognized as the seventh imam. Abu Abdallah presented Ubaidallah to the Berbers as the *mahdi* (the rightly guided one) who would inaugurate an era of peace and justice under the legitimate leadership of Ali's descendants. Fighting on his behalf, the Berbers won a string of victories along Ifriqiya's western frontier, including some in the Mzab, the Aghlabids' original territory. These successes swelled the Shii ranks, often with tribespeople motivated more by materialistic concerns than questions of Islamic legitimacy. The Aghlabids hesitated to seek the aid of Baghdad, fearing that the Abbasids might take advantage of their weakness to reassert direct control over Ifriqiya. In reality, however, the caliphs faced too many challenges to their authority closer to home to have either the inclination or the ability to intervene forcefully in the Maghrib. The rout of the Aghlabid army at al-Urbus in 909 signaled the end of the dynasty. Ziyadat Allah III fled to Egypt, leaving Ifriqiya open to his enemies.

The Aghlabid efforts to build a viable autonomous state floundered because of the dynasty's failure to seize the opportunities to link itself with the people of Ifriqiya. The overseas campaigns spared the province the turmoil that the fragmented, tribalized army might have wrought had it been permitted to concentrate its energies on the domestic political arena. They also supplied the revenue for the economic development of the region. But the ill-considered practices of Ibrahim II weakened the ties between rulers and ruled. To many of their subjects, the amirs' extravagant lifestyle, symbolized by Raqqada, emphasized their lack of interest in the populace. When an alternative to the Aghlabids arose, many of these same people, especially the Berber Muslim tribespeople on the society's fringes, supported it. Yet Shii doctrines and rituals never took root in Ifriqiya, suggesting that the movement's attraction rested primarily on the framework it provided for political protest. Irritation with the amirs of Raqqada had grown so acute that any force capable of ousting them—even one based on an interpretation of Islam not widely accepted in Ifriqiya—gained followers. The Aghlabids fell because Abu Abdallah's Berber forces repeatedly defeated them on the battlefield, but a more fundamental cause of their collapse lay in their subjects' conviction that they had nothing to lose and perhaps much to gain in any political restructuring of the province.

THE FATIMID DYNASTY, 909–973

Ubaidallah entered Ifriqiya in triumph in 910, but he showed little interest in the province itself. Not content with a niche on the periphery of the Muslim world, the mahdi sought to create a universal Shii Muslim state. The Abbasids constituted the primary obstacle to this task, and Ubaidallah lost no time laying down the gauntlet. He asserted his claim to the leadership of all Muslims by taking the title of caliph. The dynasty he established was called Fatimid, stressing its legitimation by its descent from Fatima, Muhammad's daughter and Ali's wife. As early as 913, Fatimid troops began exploratory probes into the important Abbasid province of Egypt.

The imposition of policies detrimental to the very tribespeople who had brought him to power underscored Ubaidallah's lack of concern for Ifriqiya. The first sign of a falling out came when the Kutama tribe of Berbers, the heart of Abu Abdallah's forces, were denied the opportunity to plunder the province. The Kutama viewed the wealth of the settled lands as booty, but to the Fatimids it represented their economic base. The taxes they levied, primarily to finance the large army Ubaidallah's ambitious plans necessitated, proved at least as burdensome as those of the Aghlabids. Indeed, the mahdi often applied the same taxes that Abu Abdallah had criticized when rallying tribal backing. Moreover, the new regime's insistence on Shii tenets, particularly the primacy of Ali and his descendants, irked the egalitarian Berbers.

Their disillusion peaked when Ubaidallah, fearful of Abu Abdallah's influence among the Berbers, ordered his assassination in 911. Many Kutama revolted, and other Fatimid opponents joined them. The merchants of Ifriqiya used this occasion to air their resentment of the Fatimid takeover of lucrative trade routes from the Middle East and sub-Saharan Africa, and an Aghlabid pretender on Sicily tried to capitalize on the disorders to restore the dynasty. The mahdi contained the uprising by purchasing the loyalty of many tribespeople with promises of looting in the settled areas. The ensuing sack of Kairouan guaranteed that Ubaidallah would never have the support of that important religious center, although even before the Berber attack its ulama had shown no inclination to renounce their Sunni traditions. Shii Islam made little headway either among them or the general population.

The hostility of Kairouan and the Fatimids' interests beyond Ifriqiya explain Ubaidallah's decision to construct a new capital. Mahdiyya (the city of the mahdi) lay on a peninsula jutting into the Mediterranean from the province's eastern coast. Thus the Shii rulers replaced Kairouan, founded on the desert's edge as a base for expansion farther west, with Mahdiyya, a new city on the edge of the sea, looking east to the Muslim heartlands where the Fatimids hoped to establish their ideal state.

The Fatimids did not, however, intend to ignore North Africa. Soon after checking the Kutama revolt, Ubaidallah encouraged the Berber tribes to participate in a series of military expeditions in the central and western Maghrib. He launched this campaign partly to provide an outlet for Berber activism but also to enable him to pursue his ambitions in the Islamic heartlands free from the threat of disturbances in his rear. Moreover, Fatimid control of additional North African termini of the trans-Saharan trade would bring increased revenues to finance the state he envisioned in the east. The Muslim rulers of Spain, descendants of the Umayyads who had once ruled the entire Muslim world from Damascus, also understood the potential wealth of the North African commercial centers. They attempted to halt Fatimid expansion, turning much of the Maghrib into a battlefield fought over by the Berber proxies of the two dynasties. The Fatimids, relying on Sanhaja Berbers, the broad grouping to which the Kutama belonged, prevailed, extending their control to parts of modern Algeria and Morocco by the mid-tenth century.

A resurgence of Kharajism, its appeal sharpened by the animosity many in Ifriqiya harbored for the Fatimids, coincided with this extension of their influence. A populist figure named Abu Yazid led a Kharajite insurrection around Tozeur in the Jarid shortly after the mahdi's death in 934. Realizing the danger of such a disturbance when their own resources were already stretched thin, the Fatimids quickly arrested Abu Yazid. He escaped, however, and fled to the central Maghrib, the site of several Kharajite centers dating from earlier revolts against the Arab conquerors. Within a decade, Abu Yazid renewed his campaign, capturing Tunis and Kairouan but failing to take Mahdiyya. His defeat before the Fatimid capital broke the revolt, and Abu Yazid again fled. Fatimid troops captured and executed him in 947. His death ended the Kharajite menace to Ifriqiya, but the difficulties he had caused spurred the Fatimid leaders to begin planning the complicated process of transplanting their regime to the east.

Fatimid military successes in the Nile Valley allowed the dynasty to transfer its capital to the newly created city of al-Qahira (Cairo) in 969. Although the period of Fatimid domination in Ifriqiya ended when the court left Mahdiyya four years later, the caliphs technically did not renounce their interests in the region. Buluggin ibn Ziri, the leader of a Sanhaja Berber tribe from the central Maghrib and a long-time ally, was appointed governor of Ifriqiya and the west. His primary task was to hold the Fatimid line against Spanish Umayyad and Zanata Berber aggression. Given the Fatimids' priorities and their physical distance from the Maghrib, however, this policy amounted to the gradual abandonment of Ifriqiya and paved the way for several centuries of Berber domination.

Since the conquests of the mid-seventh century, an Arab elite had held Ifriqiya in an orbit revolving around the Middle Eastern Islamic heartland. The Fatimids not only sought to break out of this orbit but to subordinate the traditional centers of Muslim political and religious authority to a Shii Islamic order of their own devising. Ifriqiya's peripheral position and the dissatisfaction of many Berber Muslims with Arab rule made the area ripe for Fatimid propaganda and, after the dynasty assumed control, an ideal springboard for its ambitions. The Fatimids used Ifriqiya's human and material resources, not least of which were the handsome profits of the trans-Mediterranean and trans-Saharan trade that the Aghlabids had promoted, to bolster their position, but they never intended to remain permanently in North Africa. Despite the initial Fatimid success in playing on anti-Aghlabid sentiments, the Berbers' distaste for alien rule did not diminish under their leadership. The Kharajite reaction, coming at a time of economic prosperity and expansion, demonstrated the fragility of the Shii hold and encouraged the implementation of the Fatimids' broader, extra-Maghribi strategy. As these grander plans increasingly preoccupied the Fatimids, their Zirid "trustees" embarked upon the venture of establishing a North African Muslim state geared to the interests of its Berber majority.

NOTES

1. Mohamed Talbi, *L'Emirat aghlabide* (Paris: Adrien-Maisonneuve, 1966), p. 22, estimated their number at fewer than 100,000 during the first century of Muslim rule.

4

Berber Dynasties

THE ZIRIDS, 973–1160

For some time after the Fatimid departure, Buluggin and his successors engaged their former masters in a cat-and-mouse game testing the limits of their independence and their legitimacy apart from their status as Fatimid agents. The Fatimids were unwilling to incur heavy expenses in curbing Zirid ambitions, but they were also unprepared simply to hand over their former territories to their vassals. They encouraged the Kutama Berbers, their original North African allies, to revolt, preventing the Zirids from focusing too sharply on their relationship with Cairo. The Fatimids' reluctance to participate in an internal Zirid dispute early in the eleventh century, however, revealed their decision to let events in Ifriqiya run their course.

When Buluggin died in 984, his relatives divided the extensive Fatimid inheritance. Hammad, Buluggin's son, received the lands of the central Maghrib just west of Ifriqiya. An attempt in 1016 by other members of the family to deprive Hammad of his domain provoked a civil war that ended with the creation of a separate Hammadid state. Their confinement to Ifriqiya proper actually enhanced the Zirids' security, for the Hammadids provided a barrier against Zanata Berber and Spanish Umayyad attacks. With the threat of direct Fatimid intervention simultaneously waning, Muiz, the Zirid amir after the war, orchestrated affairs in Ifriqiya much more easily than had his predecessors.

Cognizant of the depth of anti-Shii sentiment among many of his subjects, Muiz sought support from the influential Maliki ulama of Kairouan. Soon after assuming power, he permitted a frenzied slaughter of Shia throughout Ifriqiya. For the duration of his reign, he lavished attention on the mosque of Sidi Uqba in Kairouan and generally indulged the Sunni Muslims whom the Fatimids had at best ignored. In 1049, Muiz gave his allegiance to the Abbasid caliph, formally severing Ifriqiya's links with the Fatimids. The greater than

thirty-year interval between his accession and his break with Cairo
raises questions about Muiz's commitment to independence. Had he
acted earlier, he might have won the backing of the Maliki ulama
who, despite his show of concern, were never enthusiastic about him.
Like his predecessors, he worried that Zirid legitimacy was too closely
linked with the Fatimids to survive a total rupture. In the end, politics
only partially explains the events of 1049. Equally important in
prodding Muiz to act was the deteriorating economic condition of
Ifriqiya.

The Zirids inherited a thriving agricultural and commercial
economy from the Fatimids, and the early amirs understood the
importance of stability and the maintenance of control over the existing
caravan routes if the Fatimid departure were not to lead to economic
disruption. Their efforts in this regard won them the support of the
urban artisans and businesspeople dependent on agriculture and
commerce for their livelihoods. By retaining the Fatimid tax structure
but utilizing its considerable revenues in Ifriqiya rather than on
external projects, the Zirids reinforced a sense of economic well-being.
Grain and olive production flourished, and in the cities weavers,
metalworkers, potters, and other artisans prospered. The most active
urban center was Mansuriyya, a Fatimid-built suburb of Kairouan
used by the Zirids as their economic and political hub.

Early in the eleventh century, however, the trans-Saharan trade
began to decline. The Zirids simply could not provide the same
stimulation for this trade as had the Fatimids, who demanded its
gold and other luxury items to finance their ambitious plans and its
slaves to fill the ranks of their army. More basic to the trade's decline,
however, were the rise of the al-Murabit confederation in the western
Maghrib and the continuing sub-Saharan commercial interests of the
Fatimids themselves, both of which diverted caravan routes from
Kairouan, the traditional center of the trade in Ifriqiya. Sporadic
outbreaks of dissidence in the Jarid, with its numerous Kharajite
merchants, also disrupted commerce bound for Zirid-controlled areas.

The degeneration of the caravan trade prompted an effort to
revive Mediterranean commerce. Although not yet satisfactory commercial alternatives to the interior communities, the coastal cities
worked to ensure their own survival independent of the fate of
Kairouan. Ifriqiya was becoming a collection of communities without
central direction or a unified economy, a state of affairs particularly
damaging to Kairouan, whose basic raison d'être had been to serve
as the political and religious capital of a highly centralized state. As
such, trade and industry naturally developed there, but, stripped of
that function, Kairouan had no economic reason to exist. Its decline

caused widespread suffering, affecting not only townspeople but also the neighboring rural inhabitants whose prosperity was linked to that of the city. Peasant unrest, reminiscent of the disorders that had ended in the Donatist and Kharajite uprisings, smoldered in the Kairouan region and spread to other parts of Ifriqiya.

These economic disorders, in conjunction with Muiz's political aspirations, caused the final break with the Fatimids. Desperate for revenue, the amir confiscated vast fortunes after outlawing Fatimid coinage in Ifriqiya in 1049. The Zirids began minting their own coins to symbolize their sovereignty, and the break ended any further need for a show of deference toward Fatimid trade routes in the Sahara.

Although their vassals' disloyalty did not entirely surprise the Fatimids, they nonetheless felt obliged to respond. In forcing a group of Arab bedouin tribes, the Banu Hilal, to migrate from Upper Egypt to Ifriqiya, they rid the Nile Valley of as many as a quarter of a million nomads and unleased their energies, so disruptive to agriculture, on Ifriqiya as a punishment. When the Banu Hilal first trickled into Ifriqiya, the Zirids tried to incorporate them into the army, hoping to use the bedouins to quell disorders in rural areas precipitated by the deteriorating economy. The Zirid decision to ally with the bedouins rather than rally resistance to them indicates the magnitude of the gap between the rulers and the populace. Some Hilali tribespeople did enter Zirid service, but the amirs could not confine the rest to the peripheries of their territory. As they encroached on the settled lands, the Zirids had to mount a defense. In a pitched battle in 1052 at Haidaran, northwest of Kairouan, the Banu Hilal routed the Zirid forces, eliminating the only obstacle to their dispersal throughout Ifriqiya. Banu Hilal pressure on the Zirids continued, culminating with the sack of Kairouan in 1057.

Students of the Maghrib have long debated the consequences of this invasion. Ibn Khaldun, the fourteenth-century Tunisian scholar, compared the bedouins to a swarm of locusts destroying everything in their path while showing particular contempt for sedentary, civilized society. More recent research presents a less harsh view.[1] Disorders did, indeed, characterize eleventh-century Ifriqiya, and although the Banu Hilal took advantage of this situation, they were neither its sole nor its primary cause. Economic decline predated their appearance, and it, rather than nomadic depredations, led to the ruin of Kairouan. The spread of nomadism in the Kairouan region after 1057 sealed an already determined fate. The bedouins never controlled any important urban center, including Kairouan, for any significant period, and many smaller provincial cities actually prospered at this time, since Kairouan's collapse compelled them to explore new economic horizons.

This is not to argue that the Banu Hilal had no impact. Their presence multiplied the number of nomads in Ifriqiya, inevitably menacing agricultural life, especially in the interior. In the areas most seriously affected, some previously sedentary Berbers turned to nomadism themselves. Second, the Banu Hilal swelled Ifriqiya's small Arab population, although they were not so numerous that they altered the majority status of the Berbers. This second Arab invasion, however, made the Arab customs and traditions that had overlaid Ifriqiya since the seventh century much more apparent. No general process of Arabization yet developed, but more Berbers were more intensively exposed to more Arabs than ever before. Finally, the bedouins' mastery of large areas of the deserts and the steppes combined with the already precarious conditions of the trans-Saharan trade to transfer the commercial focus of both the Zirids and the Hammadids from the interior of Africa to the Mediterranean. The transfer of the Zirid capital to Mahdiyya after the sack of Kairouan indicated this reorientation.

The strategy might have revived Zirid fortunes had it not coincided with a resurgence of Christian power in the central Mediterranean, exemplified by Norman adventurers securing a foothold on Sicily. The island's Muslims had approached the Zirids for help early in the 1050s, but preoccupation with the Banu Hilal kept them from rendering any assistance. Although the Fatimids had specifically excluded Sicily from Zirid administration, the inability of Ifriqiya's rulers to aid their Muslim neighbors when they came under infidel attack constituted another blow to their prestige. After taking up residence in Mahdiyya, the Zirid amirs dispatched vessels to raid Christian ports and disrupt commerce throughout the central Mediterranean. Genoa and Pisa, emerging as commercial centers, could not tolerate such insecurity along their trading routes. In 1087, with the approval of the Papacy, they captured Mahdiyya,[2] which they returned to the Zirids only upon payment of a ransom. A pattern of attack and counterattack took shape as states on the northern shore of the Mediterranean demonstrated, for the first time since the Roman era, their ability to exert influence in Ifriqiya.

The Zirids' failure to master the situation either in Ifriqiya or on the high seas ensured the demise of the dynasty, although it managed to survive until the mid-twelfth century. In their weakness, the last Zirid amirs dealt with recurrent emergencies by contracting haphazard alliances that met their immediate needs but jeopardized their future. In the 1120s, for example, to counter the natural linkage that had developed between the dynasty's two major opponents, the Arabs and the Normans, the Zirids turned to the Berber al-Murabit confederation controlling much of the western Maghrib and Spain. This increased Norman pressure on Ifriqiya, which the Christians had no wish to see converted into an al-Murabit protectorate certain to pose more of a challenge than the incapacitated Zirid state they were facing. In the following decade, the Zirids relied on these same Normans and on the Arab nomads as well to protect them from a Hammadid offensive. By this marriage of convenience the Christians hoped to strengthen their position on the African coast. In 1148, the Normans turned on their Zirid allies, again seized Mahdiyya, and soon held all Ifriqiya except Tunis. The pathetic amir sought refuge in Bajaia, the capital of his Hammadid kinfolk, whose attack had prompted him to ally with the Normans in the first place.

The Zirid collapse deprived Ifriqiya of a central government capable of directing resistance to the Normans, but a popular uprising in the 1150s revealed the depth of local animosity toward the Christian occupiers. Ifriqiya's Muslims implored the al-Muwahhid dynasty, successor of the al-Murabits in the western Maghrib, to protect them from the Christians. The al-Muwahhids, already playing such a role in Spain, willingly obliged. They recaptured Mahdiyya in 1159 but chose to make Tunis the capital of the region, which they annexed to their empire. Ifriqiya diminished in importance as, for the first time in its history, it became a dependency of a state to its west.

Political relations with their Fatimid overlords concerned the Zirid amirs from the outset, but economic, rather than political, considerations triggered the chain of events that proved most crucial in the Zirid era. Shifting patterns of commerce around Ifriqiya during the first century of their rule had weakened the state's economy and eventually convinced its rulers that only a break with the Fatimids would restore economic order. But by then the deterioration was too far advanced. The influx of the Banu Hilal, deliberately sent by the Fatimids to compound the region's problems, overwhelmed the Zirids, whereas the chaotic economic situation heightened the nomads' impact. Despite this gloomy picture, the Zirids might have surmounted their difficulties by reorienting Ifriqiya's economic focus. They understood this necessity and turned to the sea in the hope of stimulating a revival. Perhaps the ease with which these Berber mountaineers did so suggests how close to the surface of Ifriqiya's collective subconscience lay the concept of a society centering on the Mediterranean. The simultaneous upswing in Christian activity in the central Mediterranean, however, stifled the chances of this approach succeeding. Reeling from economic disorders and beset by enemies on all sides, the Zirid state slowly crumbled, and its Christian and Muslim rivals shared the remnants.

IFRIQIYA AS AN AL-MUWAHHID PROVINCE, 1160–1227

While nomadic Arab tribes had been filtering into Ifriqiya, a similar process had been under way in the western Maghrib. There, however, the new arrivals were Berber, not Arab, nomads. The al-Murabit dynasty had founded Marrakesh in 1062, rapidly bringing the remainder of Morocco and parts of the Iberian peninsula under its wing. A second Berber confederation, the al-Muwahhids, unseated the al-Murabits in 1147. Driven by a desire to defend Muslim territory and spread his puritanical version of the faith, the al-Muwahhid caliph, Abd al-Mumin, embarked on a series of military expeditions in the Maghrib and Spain culminating in the annexation of Ifriqiya. Abd al-Mumin briefly presided over a unified North African empire— the first and last in its history under indigenous rule. But the very size of their holdings and the stepped up attacks of the Spanish Christians made it virtually impossible for the al-Muwahhids to keep their empire intact.

Ifriqiya proved to be one of its most troublesome provinces. Although relieved to have found a protector against the Christians, the tribes feared that al-Muwahhid rule would compromise their independence. Abd al-Mumin aggravated this mistrust by deporting some bedouin tribes to Morocco, ostensibly for service in the continuing wars in Iberia but in reality to keep them under closer surveillance. The policy backfired, fanning revolts rather than preventing them. The caliph's death in 1184 opened a prolonged period of instability throughout Ifriqiya.

A group of al-Murabit loyalists, the Banu Ghaniya, caused the greatest difficulty. From his base in the Balearic Islands, Ali ibn Ghaniya captured Bajaia and rallied the remnants of the Hammadid dynasty against their al-Muwahhid conquerors. When Bajaia was reclaimed by a quick counterattack, Ali retreated into the Jarid, where he set up his new headquarters. His attempt to unify the Arab and Berber tribes of southern Ifriqiya floundered in 1188, however, when al-Muwahhid troops again defeated him. More serious threats from Spain prevented the dynasty from stationing in Ifriqiya a force strong enough to maintain order there. No sooner had the victors withdrawn than Ali's brother, Yahya ibn Ghaniya, restarted the offensive, capturing Tunis in 1203. Although these events must have been disturbing to the al-Muwahhids, they could not turn their attention to them until

Village street. (Photo courtesy of Lewis B. Ware)

they had achieved a measure of stability in Iberia. Not until 1205 did Abd al-Wahid ibn Abi Hafs, a powerful al-Muwahhid general, march into Ifriqiya and drive Yahya from Tunis. Increasingly isolated and with his tribal support dwindling, Yahya nevertheless remained a thorn in the side of the al-Muwahhids until his death in 1238.

A stalemate had developed. On one hand, the al-Muwahhids could not check the centrifugal tendencies of Ifriqiya's tribes—a legacy of the disorders of the late Zirid period. The Banu Ghaniya, on the other hand, though taking advantage of Ifriqiya's distance from the most important al-Muwahhid centers of power to harass their enemies, had no hope of toppling them. In the long run, the most important aspect of the al-Muwahhid era for Ifriqiya was the continuing developing of the Mediterranean commerce inaugurated by the Zirids. The al-Muwahhids fought Christian expansion in Africa but were not opposed to increasing trade. They permitted European nations to appoint consuls, often themselves merchants, to represent them in North Africa. Guarantees of security for foreign businesspeople, permission for them to build residences and warehouses (*funduqs*), and the establishment of fixed import and export tariffs promoted trans-Mediterranean commerce. Dates, oil, wool, leather, and grains led Ifriqiya's exports, whereas the Europeans supplied glass, paper, dyes, wood, and metal products. The balance of trade probably favored Ifriqiya, but Europe's more advanced maritime skills left a disproportionate share of the business in the hands of merchants from Genoa, Pisa, and Marseilles.

THE HAFSID DYNASTY, 1227–1574

Abd al-Wahid ibn Abi Hafs remained governor of Ifriqiya until his death in 1221. For many years, the Hafsid family had enjoyed considerable influence among the al-Muwahhid elite. Abd al-Wahid's rivals in Marrakesh, fearing the establishment of an independent power base in Ifriqiya, dashed his hopes of turning the governorship into a hereditary office by securing the appointment of a descendant of Abd al-Mumin as his successor in Tunis. In less than a decade, however, Abd al-Wahid's son, Abu Zakariyya, had assumed his father's former position.

Abu Zakariyya's accession coincided with the most acute period of disarray the al-Muwahhids had yet experienced. Exhausted by prolonged warfare in Spain and territorially overextended in the Maghrib, the empire fragmented. Only in Morocco did the dynasty exercise real control. Many North African Muslims attributed this political and military decline to the behavior of the al-Muwahhid leaders who, they believed, were abandoning the religious puritanism that had inspired the early caliphs. Abu Zakariyya, in contrast, vigorously defended al-Muwahhid "orthodoxy," even to the point of ordering prayers in Tunisia[3] said in his own name rather than the caliph's. Such assertiveness gave the area the specific identity it had lacked since the departure of the Fatimids.

A string of military successes added to the strength and popularity of Abu Zakariyya. With great skill, he played the Tunisian tribes off against each other, facilitating their control by his soldiers, most of whom were Moroccan tribal retainers of the Hafsid family. He also integrated some local nomadic tribes into the army to forge links with the Tunisian Arabs. Stability at home enabled Abu Zakariyya to eliminate the Banu Ghaniya in 1234, absorb the Hammadid state shortly thereafter, and extend his influence as far west as Tlemcen, which he seized in 1242 from the Abd al-Wadids, another al-Muwahhid splinter group. Before he died in 1249, most inhabitants of the Maghrib and those parts of Spain still in Muslim hands had recognized Abu Zakariyya as the only effective Muslim leader in the region. Spanish Muslims appealed to Tunis for aid in stemming the tide of the Reconquest. Abu Zakariyya was reluctant to launch a major expedition across the Mediterranean, but he did encourage the resistance of Andalusian Muslims, welcoming them to Tunis when they were forced to flee their homes. The amir took many of these refugees into his bureaucracy and army, and others farmed land around new villages they established, especially in the Majarda Valley. Although the al-Muwahhid tribespeople bristled at the special treatment accorded the Andalusians, the latter formed a dynamic element in the society. Their talents for government, agriculture, crafts, and the arts contributed greatly to the prosperity Tunisia enjoyed under Abu Zakariyya.

His son and successor, Abu Abdallah, consolidated his accomplishments. In 1253, he underscored Hafsid supremacy in North Africa by taking the title of caliph, adopting the throne name al-Mustansir.[4] After the Mongols executed the Abbasid caliph and his family a few years later, prominent Muslims in Mecca and Cairo briefly acknowledged al-Mustansir's claim. But as the Mongol threat receded and a new political order emerged in the Middle East, support for al-Mustansir waned, especially in Egypt where a "shadow caliphate" headed by a distant survivor of the Abbasids emerged. Al-Mustansir could not alter geographical realities. The Maghrib remained at the periphery of the Muslim world, its leaders unable to assert permanent spiritual or secular control over the Islamic heartlands.

The Hafsids' development of a viable state disturbed their Christian neighbors, as King (later Saint) Louis IX of France demonstrated by his invasion of Tunisia in 1270. Despite the usual portrayal of the campaign as part of the ongoing effort to regain formerly Christian territory, a complex web of political, economic, and religious circumstances precipitated it. Charles of Anjou, Louis's brother, had controlled Sicily since 1266 but had failed to extract from al-Mustansir the tribute payments his father had made to Sicily's Norman rulers to protect Tunisian commerce. Al-Mustansir's hesitancy provided Louis with the excuse for an attack, but Charles, more interested in extending his control to the Byzantine lands of the eastern Mediterranean, counseled his more impetuous brother to reach a negotiated settlement with the Hafsids. Such restraint did not accord with Louis's plans. He regarded Tunisia as an excellent point of departure for a crusade he was determined to undertake against Egypt. Moreover, a strong Hafsid state in the central Mediterranean would jeopardize the communication and supply lines of any Western European crusade in the East.

Louis's forces landed at Carthage, but before the arrival of Charles and his troops, which were to round out the army, dysentery ravaged the French ranks, taking many lives, including the king's. Upon assuming command, Charles immediately arranged a peace with al-Mustansir. Despite the caliph's obvious advantage, he feared that the nomadic tribespeople who constituted the bulk of his forces would desert to care for their flocks as winter approached. The treaty guaranteed religious freedom for Christians in North Africa and imposed an indemnity that al-Mustansir agreed to pay because he saw no other way of preventing renewed Christian invasions. A subsequent upsurge in commerce justified his decision and more than compensated for the indemnity. However, the relatively weak Hafsid response to the crusade tempted other European states to meddle in Tunisian affairs.

Hafsid Decline and Revival

European interference, family rivalries, and the growing power of the Arab tribes spawned an era of instability in the century after the Hafsids turned back the crusaders. A revolt among the al-Muwahhid tribes around Bajaia in 1279, provoked by the Hafsids' reliance on Andalusian Muslims, deposed al-Mustansir's heir in favor of another member of the family. The rulers of Aragon, locked in a contest with Charles of Anjou over Sicily, supported the coup in the hope of wooing the new caliph to their views. When this did not occur, the Aragonese encouraged a second coup in 1282.

The turmoil amplified the influence of the nomadic Arab tribes. Since the Hilali invasion of the eleventh century, another large group of bedouins, the Banu Sulaim, had migrated to Tunisia. Hafsid contenders for power during the unsettled period following al-Mustansir's death often turned to the Arabs for support. Abu Hafs Umar, who emerged in 1284 as the victor in these struggles, had especially depended on the Banu Sulaim. Once in power, he broke with the policies of his predecessors, who had given the bedouins only monetary rewards, by bestowing on the tribal leaders *iqta*s, or land grants, in return for military service. These grants strengthened the Arabs' position by giving them a more stable economic base; at the same time, they weakened the central government by diverting funds from the treasury. As the percentage of Arabs in Hafsid service rose, the process of Arabization accelerated. Arab tribal shaikhs replaced leaders of the original al-Muwahhid tribes as local agents of the Tunis government, the use of Arabic spread, and Arabo-Berber cultural and racial distinctions became increasingly blurred.

Under certain circumstances, the Arabs could shore up the caliph's position, but their preference for autonomy made them as much a threat as an asset to the Hafsids. In any case, they provided little help to the dynasty against its European enemies. In 1284, after Aragon had wrested Sicily from Charles, it seized the island of Jarba, a useful base for controlling the central Mediterranean sealanes. But because most of the island's people were Kharajites, the Hafsids did not respond to this attack on territory at least nominally under their jurisdiction. Their inaction tempted Aragon to intrigue further, leading it into an abortive conspiracy to bring the virtually powerless al-Muwahhid caliph to power in Tunis. An uneasy Hafsid-Aragonese rapprochement came about in the 1290s with the signing of a commercial treaty that, like others the Hafsids had with Europeans, gave considerable privileges to the Christians.

Perhaps more than any other factor, however, family feuds contributed to the regime's instability. Hafsid rivals of Abu Hafs Umar established themselves in Bajaia late in the thirteenth century. At the same time, many cities in Tunisia also severed their links with the central government. Hafsid insecurity drove the caliphs into an alliance in the 1320s with the Marinids, successors of the al-Muwahhids in the western Maghrib, but this defensive strategy failed. Marinid soldiers, helped by some Arab tribes, occupied Tunis in 1346, unimpeded by the Hafsid princes who were battling each other for the vacant throne. Subsequent Marinid attempts to restrain their Arab supporters spurred a tribal revolt. The urban population, suffering terribly from an economic collapse brought on by the appearance of the Black Plague more or less simultaneously with the occupation, added its opposition, rendering the conquerors' situation untenable.

The Marinids withdrew, but Hafsid rivalries permitted them to re-capture Tunis in 1357. The Marinids again failed to master the Arabs and, facing challenges to their authority at home, withdrew.

Recurrent attacks from within Tunisia, from other quarters in the Maghrib, and from overseas convinced the Hafsids of the need for a quick and authoritative restoration of stability and confidence if they were to survive. The failure of the two Marinid bids for hegemony suggests how deeply the notion of a separate Tunisian identity had taken root, despite the shaky nature of Hafsid control. Such a notion gave Hafsid leaders a basis for the revival of the family's fortunes after the second Marinid interlude.

As the Marinid threat subsided, three Hafsid centers, Tunis, Bajaia, and Constantine, coexisted uneasily. Abu'l Abbas, the initiator of the dynasty's revitalization, first united the two western cities and then added Tunis to his holdings when Abu Ishaq, who had presided there since the end of the first Marinid occupation, died in 1370. The reign of Abu'l Abbas for almost a quarter of a century was followed by the even longer rules of Abu Faris (1394–1434) and Uthman (1434–1488). These able men, whose longevity played no small part in their success, strengthened the army by recruiting well-trained and highly disciplined mercenaries, including both Turks and Christians. The reinvigorated military dealt aggressively with the troublesome tribes, bringing them largely—although never entirely—under the central government's control. The fifteenth-century Hafsid rulers also solidified their position by gaining the support of the ulama by abolishing non-Quranic taxes and patronizing religious institutions. The stability these three rulers brought to Tunisia paved the way for the first extension of Hafsid territory since the beginning of the dynasty. Algiers, Tlemcen, and even Marinid Fez acknowledged Hafsid supremacy in the early fifteenth century, and Hafsid support of Granada, the last remaining Muslim state in Spain, pleased the many North African Muslims of Andalusian origin. The growth of the Hafsids' domains, after a century of stagnation and fragmentation, signaled a reversal of fortunes. Success built upon success, adding to the rising prestige of Tunis's rulers.

As they gained confidence at home, the Hafsids responded more vehemently to the European domination of the central Mediterranean and its constriction of Muslim maritime horizons. Bajaia served as the headquarters of Hafsid corsairs who harried both Christian commercial vessels and the Christian corsairs who had long preyed, without fear of retribution, on Muslim shipping. An undeclared war raged throughout the fifteenth century. The European inability to suppress this challenge further enhanced Hafsid prestige in the

Maghrib. The corsairs operated independent of the state, which never developed a true navy. Nevertheless, the treasury benefited from corsairing by claiming a share of the profits from the sale of seized goods and ships, as well as a share of the ransoms extracted for captives.

Corsair activity had become so widely accepted in both Europe and Africa that it scarcely impeded the growth of commerce. Because Tunisia's role as a terminus for the trans-Saharan trade had steadily diminished, Hafsid trade with Europe at this time rested on the export of domestic agricultural products. Venice and Genoa headed the list of trading partners. Tunisia faced stiff competition in trans-Mediterranean commerce from Egyptian and Levantine ports. Those cities' easier access to the luxury goods of the East, which commanded high prices on European markets, gave them an advantage. The Hafsids benefited from the disruption of eastern Mediterranean trading patterns that accompanied the rise of the Ottoman Empire in the fourteenth century, in that many Italian merchants diverted their business to North Africa. Similarly, the instability occasioned by the Ottoman-Mamluk hostilities in Egypt and Syria early in the sixteenth century strengthened the Maghrib's commercial links with Europe.

Spanish Power in Tunisia

In the 100 years preceding Uthman's death, only three men had ruled the Hafsid state. Three more held the throne in the following decade, as family jealousies again came to the fore. This round of dynastic upheaval sealed the Hafsids' fate because it coincided with a burst of Spanish militancy directed against North Africa. The combined kingdoms of Aragon and Castile conquered Granada in 1492—a victory that fueled the desire to extend the Christian Reconquest into Africa itself. But the prospects of controlling the trans-Saharan trade and curbing Muslim corsairs motivated the Spaniards as powerfully as any religious objectives. Bajaia and Tripoli fell in 1510, and only a spirited defense engineered by a Muslim corsair from the Levant, Khair al-Din Barbarossa, saved Algiers.

Elsewhere in the Mediterranean, the projection of Ottoman power as far as Egypt in 1517 paralleled the Spanish offensive. The Ottomans were anxious to build as broad a base of Muslim support as possible. They lost no time in responding to a request for help from Khair al-Din who, after ruling Algiers as a private fief since 1510, saw new advantages in recognizing the suzerainty of the Ottoman sultan. But to the Hafsids, the Ottomans constituted merely another challenge. Although the Turks were Muslims, the rulers of Tunis assessed them as potential enemies and launched a war against Khair al-Din. Aided by Turkish troops, the latter took the offensive, seized Tunis in 1534, and deposed the Hafsid ruler.

Nothing so clearly demonstrated the Hafsids' bankruptcy as their decision to seek help from the Hapsburg Emperor Charles V, who also ruled Spain as Charles I. Spanish troops ousted the Turks and restored Tunis and its port, La Goulette, to the Hafsids in 1535. By assuming a protectorate over the debilitated monarchy, Spain assured itself of a friendly government on the narrows linking the western and eastern basins of the Mediterranean. The Hapsburgs well knew that any escalation of Ottoman-Spanish warfare would make the control of the straits between Tunisia and Sicily of the utmost importance. Muslim corsairs, equally attuned to the area's strategic significance, set about creating bases on Jarba and other former Hafsid territories during the 1540s.

Spain's vigorous response to raids by these corsairs persuaded the Ottomans that direct intervention was necessary to check the Christians in the central Mediterranean. In 1551, the Turks captured Tripoli and made Darghut, a prominent corsair, its governor. He extended his control over much of southern Tunisia, but his inept treatment of the tribes left him with little support when Spain attacked Jarba in 1560. Along with the Hafsids, some tribes rallied behind the Spanish expedition. Nevertheless, Tripoli, the main target of the offensive, held.

Tunisia formed an uneasy frontier between the Ottomans and the Spanish Hapsburgs, with neither power willing to concede the strategically important region to its rival. The Ottoman Empire's agent in Algiers, the corsair Ilj Ali, occupied Tunis in 1569, compelling the Hafsid family to flee to the safety of the Spanish fortress in La Goulette. The Hapsburgs again organized a revival. Don John of Austria, the brother of the Spanish king and a Christian hero after his naval victory over the Turks at Lepanto, helped the Hafsids to return to Tunis in 1573. But the dynasty lacked popular backing. In 1574, an Ottoman fleet evicted the Hapsburgs from La Goulette and deposed the Hafsids, clearing the way for an Ottoman assumption of power in Tunisia.

Emergence of a Tunisian Identity

Despite its origins among the Berber tribes of the western Maghrib, the Hafsid family presided over the emergence of a distinctive Tunisian identity more Arab than Berber. Circumstances in the mid-thirteenth-century Muslim world combined to ensure far greater influence for the first Hafsids, both within the Maghrib and beyond it, than for any previous rulers in Tunisia. The dynasty's early successes bred jealousies and family rivalries, plunging the state into turmoil. To protect themselves, Hafsid monarchs forged alliances with Arab nomads, eventually allowing the latter to supplant the al-Muwahhid tribes as the mainstay of their army. Thereafter, the pace of Arabization quickened. Arab resistance to outside domination foiled both Marinid attempts to take advantage of Tunisian instability in the fourteenth century, but central control over the tribes remained shaky. Subsequent generations of Hafsid rulers strove to restrain the Arabs and balance the often conflicting interests of their subjects. When a succession of able rulers achieved such stability in the course of the fifteenth century, the Hafsid state experienced the most prosperous era in its history.

This evolutionary process required Hafsid flexibility in the very important arena of religion. Neither the Arabs nor the Andalusian refugees liked the austere al-Muwahhid interpretations of Islam. At first, the Hafsids had specifically championed those views, rejecting the Maliki traditions that had prevailed before al-Muwahhid times. But widespread Tunisian acceptance of the Maliki school, coupled with their own growing detachment from the centers of al-Muwahhid power, led the Hafsids to acknowledge its preeminence. As a result, Maliki traditions assumed an important place in the Tunisian identity taking shape under Hafsid auspices. In a related vein, the Andalusians' highly personalized concept of religion promoted the growth of sufism (Islamic mysticism) and many of its attendant practices, including a reverence for devout mystics regarded as saints. Sufism stressed attaining religious satisfaction through the believer's direct and personal contact with the divinity. It minimized the importance of the ulama and of the religious institutions associated with them. Consequently, sufism had a particularly strong appeal in times when the establishment experienced crises. During the Hafsid period, and especially as the threat posed by Christian Spain reached its height in the sixteenth century, the popularity of sufism rose.

A steady commercial intercourse with Europe was also a salient feature of the Hafsid years. Trade, which primarily benefited the Christians, persisted even in the face of crusades and European interference in Tunisian domestic affairs. The Hafsid renewal of the fifteenth century, however, challenged Christian economic and political might on the Mediterranean. Until the culmination of the Spanish Reconquest in 1492, the Hafsids fared well in holding the Europeans at bay while still engaging in commerce, but when the combined kingdoms of Aragon and Castile determined to carry the Reconquest into Africa, the Hafsids could not withstand the onslaught. The decision of Tunisia's smaller neighbors to invite the Ottomans into the region to protect them turned the entire Maghrib into a pawn in the Turks' battle with Spain for control of the Mediterranean. By accepting Spanish help against the Ottomans, the Hafsids thoroughly discredited themselves in the eyes of their subjects and succeeded only in forestalling for a few decades the inauguration of Ottoman rule.

NOTES

1. The strikingly different assessments of the Hilali impact can be explained in part by the colonial circumstances in which the French historians who devised them wrote. These scholars, deeply committed to the continuation of French rule in North Africa, sometimes projected their evaluations of the contemporary situation backward in time. French policy in the Maghrib often favored the Berbers, whom many French administrators judged more assimilable than the Arab majority, which was seen as more hostile to France and more sympathetic to the nationalist movements developing after World War I. This approach was intended to prevent the emergence of a united anticolonial front. In analyzing the eleventh-century confrontation between the Arab Banu Hilal and the Berber Zirids, some scholars painted the Arabs as unreconstructed villains, terrorizing the Berbers and destroying their achievements in much the same way that their descendants wanted to undermine France's accomplishments in North Africa. Such a bias promoted the rationalization that the Arabs had always been a destructive force in the Maghrib. Only after the colonial era ended did these unsupportable assertions give way to a more balanced and objective interpretation of the region's eleventh-century history.

2. The attack on Mahdiyya preceded, by more than a decade, the Papacy's call for the First Crusade in the Holy Land but was no less a Christian offensive against Islam. The Christian Reconquest of the Iberian peninsula, beginning at approximately the same time, is an added reminder that the effort to oust the Muslims from Jerusalem formed part of a broad Christian campaign throughout the Mediterranean Basin that hostilities between Muslims and Christians in Ifriqiya had helped to initiate.

3. With the transferral of the political center of gravity to Tunis in the al-Muwahhid era and the subsequent development of that city by the Hafsids, it seems reasonable to begin using the term *Tunisia* in preference to the previously more appropriate *Ifriqiya*.

4. The use of throne names dated to the earliest Abbasid caliphs and had been imitated by all subsequent claimants, including the Fatimids, Spanish Umayyads, and al-Muwahhids. As with the Zirid coinage of money, Muslims clearly understood the symbolism of this Hafsid gesture.

5

Ottoman and Husainid Tunisia

THE EARLY OTTOMAN ERA, 1574–1591

A Turkish military regime governed Tunisia after the deposition of the Hafsids and the ouster of their Spanish allies. An appointee of the Ottoman sultan bearing the honorific title of *pasha* exercised civil and military power in Tunis aided by several thousand Ottoman infantrymen, the janissaries. Their commanding officer, the *agha*, headed a *diwan*, or council, created to apprise the pasha of the troops' needs. The Turks emphasized Tunisia's strategic position in the Ottoman-Spanish confrontation, but their desire to defend Islam in the central Mediterranean may have outweighed economic and political concerns in the Ottomans' decision to enter the region.

The dismal performance of the last Hafsids contrasted poorly with Ottoman dynamism, and many urbanites, particularly in Tunis, welcomed the Turks as saviors. The influential ulama, for example, upheld the new rulers out of their conviction that a stable atmosphere promoted Islam whereas chaos imperiled it. In the cities, a Turkish military aristocracy, with its own ideas about government and administration, replaced the discredited Hafsids, but little else changed in the urban social order.

In the countryside, there was less enthusiasm for the Turks. The tribespeople considered them another alien occupier, and their suspicions increased as the danger of Spanish intervention receded but the Ottomans remained. Moreover, although the Hafsids had built alliances with the nomadic tribes, the Ottomans' military prowess enabled them to curb the tribes rather than placate them. An image of Turkish domination and Tunisian subordination emerged everywhere, with the split between ruler and ruled resting exclusively on race.

55

The containment of the tribes did not, however, give the Turks control of the economy of the interior, which the instability of the late Hafsid era had seriously retarded. Consequently, Tunisia's Ottoman rulers, like the Hafsids before them, relied upon corsair raiding—a pursuit far more profitable than commerce in the sixteenth-century Mediterranean world—as their major economic prop. A formal peace between the Ottomans and Spain in 1581 turned Spanish attention away from the Mediterranean, resulting in an upsurge of corsair activity.

POLITICS IN THE ERA OF THE DEYS AND BEYS, 1591-1705

Istanbul did not normally supply janissaries to the pasha. Instead, the pasha recruited his own troops from within and outside the Ottoman Empire. As a result, many of the janissaries were not Turks. A military coup in 1591, led by junior-level janissary officers called *deys*, stripped the pasha and the diwan of power. This bold act defied the Ottoman sultan and attenuated the links between Tunis and Istanbul, but foreigners, not Tunisians, continued to dominate the country. Once in control, the deys did not involve Tunisians in the administration, except for some Maliki ulama. Despite the Turks' preference for the Hanafi madhhab, Maliki officials received key slots in the religious establishment, no doubt in recognition of the importance the regime attached to their approval or at least their acquiescence. On a more practical plane, the overwhelming majority of Tunisians were Maliki and the deys saw no point in antagonizing them by forcefully imposing a different madhhab.

The deys controlled the cities with relative ease but assigned the more difficult task of maintaining order and security in rural regions to an official called the *bey*. The beys formalized an occasional practice of earlier Tunisian rulers by dispatching semiannual military expeditions, *mahallas*, among the tribes. These expeditions collected taxes but also "showed the flag" as a reminder that the deys did not view themselves strictly as an urban power. The beys also organized cavalry units drawn from groups designated as *makhzan* (government) tribes. In return for tax exemptions, these warriors, most of whom were Arabs, provided the government with an auxiliary force that could be mobilized as the need arose. Both the mahallas and the creation of the makhzan tribes helped push the limits of deylical authority south and west beyond the immediate vicinity of Tunis.

The beys' function as intermediaries between the central government and the tribes placed them in a position to challenge the deys. One highly successful bey, Murad Corso (a Corsican renegade), was also named pasha of Tunis by the sultan. He conveyed both titles to his son Hamuda (1631–1666). After the death of the ruling dey in 1640, Hamuda controlled the appointment of subsequent holders of the office. In a process guaranteeing the family's fortunes, Hamuda then began strengthening his links with the Tunis bourgeoisie, particularly the ulama. He evidently envisioned the formation of a Tunisian coalition (into which he fit by virtue of his place of birth, if not his ethnicity) against external pressures. But at the same time, he carefully maintained the appearance of subordination to Istanbul, theoretically the source of his legitimacy.

The deys realized that inaction in the face of the continued succession of Murad's heirs would confirm beylical supremacy. In 1673, they revolted against Hamuda's son, Murad II. Recalling the sometimes ruthless tactics of the beys in pacifying the countryside, some tribes aligned themselves with the deys. In general, however, the civil war pitted the rural tribes under the direction of the Tunisian beys against the "Turkish" deys and their urban-based troops, most of which were composed of janissaries. Murad II's victory ensured the preeminence of the beys. He continued to recruit soldiers from throughout the Ottoman Empire, but the confrontation between the beys and the deys had revealed the increased stature of local tribal forces. The morale and effectiveness of the regular army, with the janissaries at its center, declined, to the detriment of later Muradid rulers who found they still needed these soldiers to supplement their tribal levies.

Murad II's death in 1675 precipitated a power struggle this time not between the dey and the bey but between rivals within the Muradid family. The contenders drew heavily on the aid of tribal factions—a process underlining the growing importance of the rural regions. A victor emerged in 1680, but a few years later a competitor ousted him with the help of the Turkish rulers of Algeria. Both claimants to the throne, uncomfortably thrown together in the face of a renewed bid for power by the dey, again sought outside intervention. In 1686, janissaries from Algiers, aided by the would-be beys' tribal auxiliaries, captured Tunis. The more powerful of their Muradid allies, Muhammad, quickly eliminated his family rivals and assumed the offices of both dey and bey. Muhammad ruled until 1696, but he soon discovered the double-edged nature of his appeal to Algeria's Turks. With Tunisia's own janissaries weakened by the decades of infighting and only tribal forces on which to rely, he could not prevent the Algerians from intervening in Tunisian affairs.

Relations with Algeria soured as Muhammad distanced himself from his former sponsors. His effort to extend Tunisian control over tribes along the Algerian frontier provoked his western neighbors to drive him from his capital in 1694–1695 and create a puppet government in his stead, but the unpopularity of this foreign-imposed regime enabled Muhammad to rally opposition and overthrow it with relative ease. Antagonism toward Algeria remained an important theme of the last Muradid bey, Murad III, whose campaign against it in 1700 had broad backing. His harsh domestic policies, however, aroused resentment. He was assassinated in 1702 by Ibrahim Sharif, a Turkish member of his entourage, who also executed other members of the beylical family and briefly ruled Tunisia until the Algerians again intervened to establish a government more responsive to their interests. In opposing this episode of Algerian encroachment, Husain ibn Ali installed himself as bey, founding the dynasty that provided at least nominal leadership for Tunisia for the following two and a half centuries.

CORSAIRS AND INTERNATIONAL COMMERCE IN THE MURADID ERA, 1630–1705

The Muradid era witnessed the gradual subordination of corsair activity to peaceful commerce that depended partly on agricultural production to supply goods for trade. The bases on which the state's economy rested did not change in the seventeenth century even though the relative emphasis placed on them did.

The Turkish military rulers of Tunisia took control of corsair activity soon after 1574, although Andalusian immigrants and Christian renegades continued to figure prominently. The Turks' eagerness to engage in corsair pursuits stemmed from economic concerns. The European stranglehold on Mediterranean commerce from the eleventh through the sixteenth centuries had resulted in the systematic exclusion of North African Muslims from all but the most minimal participation in legitimate trade. At the time of the Ottoman conquest of Tunisia, corsairs provided the most reliable source of income for the treasury. As long as the Turks could not be sure of a steady flow of tax revenues from the interior, maritime raiding remained essential. The Tunisian corsair fleet never grew very large, however, since equipping ships required a substantial capital outlay.

The corsairs' most lucrative prizes were Europeans whom they could hold for ransom or, in the case of artisans or professionals, whose skills they could use in Tunis itself. Although Western perceptions of the "Barbary pirates" focused on the presumed horrors

of enslavement, the corsairs regarded their captives as valuable merchandise and treated them with the same care they would have given
to any inanimate object of great worth. Slaves' activities in Tunis
were certainly curtailed, but mistreatment was counterproductive and
instances of it were rare.

The spread of mercantilist philosophies in seventeenth-century
Europe encouraged efforts to discipline the Tunisian (and other North
African) corsairs. In 1662, England and Holland combined naval forces
to impose a treaty on the bey safeguarding their vessels. But the
power most anxious about the raiders' depredations was France. In
theory, the events of 1574 rendered the Franco-Ottoman commercial
accords, or the capitulations, applicable to Tunisia. These arrangements
should have protected the rights of merchants from each country
doing business with the other, but the rapid diminution of Ottoman
influence in Tunisia allowed the beys to ignore them. As Marseilles
merchants cornered a growing proportion of the trans-Mediterranean
trade, France forced Tunisia to accept new commercial treaties in
1665, 1672, and 1685. The last of these granted France the right to
establish a trading post at Cape Negre from which large quantitites
of wheat, the major French import from Tunisia, were shipped. A
precedent for such a territorial concession existed in Khair al-Din's
grant of the island of Tabarka, off Tunisia's northern coast, to Genoese
merchants in 1540 as a ransom for the captured corsair Darghut. The
Genoese used the island primarily as a base for coral fishing.

The corsairs' threat to European trade routes, rather than any
direct threat to Europe itself, brought the relatively sophisticated
military might of the Christian states to bear on Tunisia. Domestic
political instability in the last quarter of the century prevented the
Muradids from giving their undivided attention to this serious problem.
With corsair activities crippled, the beys sought economic compensation in the interior. But the central government still lacked the
resources necessary to manage the hinterland effectively. A succession
of poor harvests decreased the already meager revenues supplied by
the provinces, ending any hope for sustained relief from that quarter.
Deprived of other options, Tunisia found itself drawn into commercial
pursuits in an international market dominated by its enemies.

As the volume of its international trade grew, the state assumed
a paramount position by imposing itself between local producers and
foreign businesspeople. The beys established government monopolies
on the most important exports, beginning with grains, and sold
monopolies on other commodities to private investors, including a
number of Livornese Jewish merchants living in the country. The
Europeans had achieved commercial supremacy in the Mediterranean

by forcefully excluding Maghribi merchantmen from their ports. Not only did this compel the North Africans to rely on corsair activities for their share in international commerce, but it also discouraged the development of a Tunisian merchant fleet. Consequently, even when legitimate trade was expanded, most Tunisian exports moved on European vessels.

The volume of Tunisian trade with France in the late 1600s was more than triple that of Franco-Algerian business, indicating the success of the decision to try to acquire sorely needed funds through commerce. (This same statistic offers an additional explanation of Algeria's repeated attempts to control Muradid Tunisia.) Nevertheless, the system of government regulation and monopolies produced less revenue than might have been generated by a more open approach to Tunisian commerce. The quick profits and easy control afforded by the former system appealed to the beys, who ignored its serious disadvantage of permitting European capital to control international exchanges.

The initial inclination of Ottoman Tunisia's military rulers to base their economy on corsair activities minimized the likelihood of the development of either a local aristocracy based on rural land ownership or a wealthy mercantile class. Even when maritime commerce surpassed corsair raiding in economic importance, the rulers and a handful of their associates secured the lion's share of its profits, depriving Tunisian merchants of any significant role. In late sixteenth- and seventeenth-century Tunisia, a clear distinction, although not an unbridgeable gap, existed between rulers and ruled. It stemmed from the Ottoman identity and linkages of the rulers (whether or not they were Turks) and the local identity and linkages of the ruled. This situation created the framework of a social order that long outlasted the Ottomans. From the seventeenth century until well into the era of the French protectorate, the important families of Tunisia were those with some connection—economic, social, or political—with the country's "Turkish" ruling caste.

The triumph of the beys over the deys cleared the way for a certain harmonization of the interests of the rulers and the ruled. The beys' association with both the Tunisian tribes and such traditional urban forces as the ulama facilitated this process. Like the deys who preceded them, the Muradids used Ottoman terminology and institutions as symbols of their legitimacy. Unlike the deys, the Muradids involved Tunisians in the affairs of government. The use of Arabic as an administrative language spread, although the rulers themselves never dropped the use of Turkish, maintaining it to distinguish them from their subjects.

The impact of native Tunisians in the Muradid period must be kept in perspective. Few could be said to have held real power within the regime. Nevertheless, to the extent that both the use of the tribes as the beys' auxiliary forces and the entry of Tunisian urbanites into the bureaucracy eroded the monopoly on power previously enjoyed by the non-Tunisian ruling class, they contributed to the transformation of Tunisia from a city-state to a territorial one. Resistance to Algerian attempts at domination toward the end of the Muradid era came not only from the tribes customarily opposed to any form of outside control but also from the citizens of the capital, pointing to the rekindling of a national conscience, first apparent in the Hafsid era.

POLITICAL AND ECONOMIC DEVELOPMENTS UNDER HUSAINID LEADERSHIP

The Solidification of Husainid Power

Husain ibn Ali, a cavalry officer of Greek extraction in Muradid service, claimed the title of bey in 1705 after leading the Tunisian resistance to the Algerian invasion that had followed Ibrahim Sharif's coup. The urban population, led by the ulama, willingly supported Husain, seeing in him the surest counter to Algerian ambitions. When Tunisia's janissaries attempted to take advantage of the unstable political atmosphere to replace Husain with one of their leaders—a bid to revive the powers of the dey—he adopted the Muradid tactic of turning to the tribes for help, thereby further emphasizing his ties with native Tunisians. The sultan's bestowal of the title of pasha on Husain in 1708 acknowledged his position and gave him the important seal of Ottoman legitimacy. Nevetheless, Husain rebuffed an Ottoman effort to reassert direct control over Tunisia by naming a new governor in 1715. In the interim, he had secured the backing of Tunis notables not only for keeping his office but also for transmitting it within his family.

At first Husain groomed his nephew Ali as his successor, but his appointment of his fifteen-year-old son Muhammad to command the mahalla in 1724 marked a change of heart and the younger man's selection as heir apparent. The absence of any concept of primogeniture made Husain's decision perfectly legitimate, but the frustrated Ali rebelled a few years later. Both factions in the civil war recruited extensively among the Tunisian tribes, forcing them to take sides and opening rifts that lasted for at least another century. Ali defeated Husain in 1740, but because he could not reconcile the differences surrounding his rise to power his reign was a troubled one. Husain's

Weekly rural market. (Photo courtesy of Lewis B. Ware)

sons reopened the war in 1746 and returned to power with the capture of Tunis a decade later. The Turks in Algeria had assisted Ali in the 1720s, but in the second round of fighting they turned against him. Throughout the eighteenth century, they pursued a policy of promoting discord in Tunisia, keeping its monarchy off balance so as to strengthen their own influence in the country.

Husain's descendants understood the importance of a strong base of local support to offset Algerian aspirations. To gain that support, they countenanced additional Arabization in the bureaucracy, promoted economic development, and sought the approval of influential religious leaders. Throughout the Husainid period, native Tunisians and the *kouloughlis* (children of mixed Turkish and Tunisian parentage) played an increasingly important role in Tunisian society.

The early Husainids' ability to protect Tunisia from Algerian encroachments had won them the gratitude and approval of the ulama, ever conscious of the need for stability. Tunisians, trained as ulama at the Zaituna mosque-university in Tunis (and occasionally at other institutions), filled many clerical and judicial posts in the Husainid bureaucracy. The beys subsidized the ulama, showing particular enthusiasm for their efforts to build Quranic schools in the interior. This undertaking spread the high Islamic traditions of the cities into the countryside, tying it more closely to the urban-based central government and counteracting the influence of local saints, or marabouts. Still, the beys respected the powerful and popular marabouts and, in taking pains to mollify them, provided another mechanism for a few native Tunisians to influence the state system. Some tribal leaders were also admitted to the ranks of the ruling elite, but of far greater importance than any of these groups was the handful of prominent Tunisian families, often businesspeople and landowners, who served the rulers in a variety of political and economic capacities and who managed to link their fortunes to the beys' own.

Neither did the Husainids ignore their Ottoman heritage. Like the Muradids, they believed that their connection with the empire heightened their legitimacy, but they carefully kept their distance from Istanbul to avoid any appearance of welcoming a reassertion of imperial authority. The Husainid beys continued to recruit janissaries from the Ottoman lands to shore up their tribal forces, but a revolt in 1811 convinced Hamuda Bey (1782–1814) to decrease the janissary corps from roughly 4,000 to 3,000 and to increase the number of Zwawa Berber tribespeople in the regular military establishment.

Of far greater long-term significance regarding ties with the empire was the Husainid practice of purchasing on Ottoman markets non-Muslim slave youths called *mamluk*s. The beys educated these young men along with the scions of the royal family. Their regimen included religious training, culminating in their conversion to Islam, and instruction to prepare them for important administrative responsibilities in the government. Mamluks rose in the hierarchy to the uppermost echelons of the central and provincial government. Rarely numbering more than 100, the mamluks enjoyed enormous power by virtue of their proximity and loyalty to the rulers with whom they usually had grown up. The beys preferred to marry their daughters to the mamluks; despite the Husainids' overtures to the Tunisians, they rarely showed any interest in establishing marital bonds with them. The dynasty never ceased to identify itself as an Ottoman, not an indigenous, elite.

An Unstable Economy

The economy of the Husainid era rested on Tunisia's continuing involvement in international trade, which in turn provided a stimulus to domestic production. During the 1700s, growing numbers of Tunisians participated in the Mediterranean monetary economy, many for the first time. Olive growers in the Sahil, for example, began to export substantial quantities of oil. Producers of cereals and hides also sold for export, thus inextricably linking their economic fate to the fluctuations of the broader Mediterranean market. Some Tunisian artisans, such as the manufacturers of *shashiyas* (brimless red woolen caps traditionally worn by Muslim males) and cloth goods, developed new international trade networks, with shashiya makers even depending on the importation of raw materials for the fabrication of their product. Other Tunisians served in the international economy as middlemen in the Saharan trade that, although much less profitable than its heyday, still remained viable. In addition to engaging directly in overseas commerce, some Tunisian merchants acted as intermediaries between producers and buyers for commodities over which the government did not exercise a monopoly. In this way, they benefited from the gap between the low prices of goods on rural markets and the relatively high sums they commanded in foreign trade. One venture in which private businesspeople and the beys and their entourages all invested was corsair activity, although its decline in the 1700s decreased its attractiveness.

A combination of inclement weather, poor harvests, and recurrences of plague occasioned an economic slump in the last quarter of the eighteenth century. Only the simultaneous outbreak of political upheavals in Europe alleviated the country's distress. The French Revolutionary and Napoleonic Wars disrupted the European economy, creating increased demand for Tunisian goods and elevating the prices they commanded. Because French and Italian merchants were unable to operate freely on the Mediterranean, North Africans, including Tunisians, took their places. These disruptions also led to a resurgence of corsair activity. With the powers unable to police the sea effectively, Tunisian raiding briefly reached the same intensity it had attained at its height in the seventeenth century. Hamuda Bey, who presided over the Tunisian recovery of the early 1800s, won the loyalty of the many Tunisians who prospered from this chain of events, as demonstrated by the popular support he enjoyed in the face of an unsuccessful Algerian invasion in 1807 and a janissary revolt in 1811.

Hamuda's death in 1814 opened a violent power struggle between rival branches of the Husainid family and their retainers. The weakness of Hamuda's successors (Uthman, 1814; Mahmud, 1814–1824; and Husain, 1824–1835) gave the Europeans an opportunity to take the political and economic offensive after 1815. The powers began by curbing the corsairs. A British naval expedition under the command of Lord Exmouth bombarded Tunis (and other Maghribi ports from which corsairs had operated) in 1816, and in 1819 a joint Anglo-French fleet compelled the bey to adhere to the terms of the Treaty of Aix-la-Chapelle outlawing corsair activity. Except during a few years of the Greek revolution, the practice was never revived. By that time, it had already become an economically marginal activity, practical only under certain abnormal circumstances. Its termination did not seriously hurt the state's economy.

Almost three-fourths of the beylical government's revenues traditionally came from taxes on agricultural products. Consequently, several woefully inadequate harvests, followed by widespread famine and disease that further debilitated the rural populace, proved much more damaging than the cessation of corsair raids.[1] These agrarian troubles corresponded with a decline in Tunisian commerce and industry. The depression that gripped Europe after the Napoleonic Wars lessened the demand for, and the value of, Tunisian goods. Throughout the 1820s, the cost of imports doubled, and the tendency of Mahmud Bey and his closest associates to make substantial credit purchases of European luxury goods pointed the way. In the same decade, the value of exports rose by less than 50 percent.[2] Moreover, the export of manufactured products that had been important revenue earners, including shashiyas, virtually ended because of increased competition and, in the case of shashiyas, the prohibitive cost of imported materials. To meet the increasing demands of foreign creditors, Mahmud sold Tunisian goods at less than optimum prices. As Tunisian monetary reserves dwindled, European merchants, who had greater financial liquidity made loans, often at usurious rates, to Tunisians who saw such arrangements as their only hope of staying afloat. European businesspeople increasingly controlled Tunisia's export trade.

The beys experimented with reforms they hoped would halt the economic slide. An 1824 effort to devalue the piastre failed when speculators hoarded the old coins and new ones were minted so slowly that severe shortages lasted for several years, worsening rather than improving the situation. In a time of already declining production, higher taxes resulted in little additional state revenue but did succeed in provoking rural revolts. The ties with the countryside that the Husainids had built up over the years were on the verge of breaking down. Even the government's traditional tactic of buying cheaply from peasant producers and selling dear on the international market was of no avail. Olives were then Tunisia's most valuable commodity, and in 1819 the government required olive growers to pay their taxes in kind to ensure that the government had a good supply of this marketable commodity. In the 1820s, the government instituted a formal monopoly on olives. The bey customarily sold the oil to foreign merchants in advance of the harvest. The dangers of such speculation surfaced in 1828 when the harvest failed and the government could not fulfill its commitments. The bey had no choice but to meet his contractual obligations by purchasing oil on the international market at a grossly inflated price, thereby assuming a debt to French business interests of over 2 million francs.

Despite the urgency of the crisis, the government never tightened its belt. The bey and his court associates continued to spend freely, often on impractical luxury items, driving Tunisia's international debt higher and higher. Private merchants and businesspeople, whose desire to emulate the royal entourage gave them a taste for imported goods they could not afford, increasingly depended on the credit of the European merchants who already dominated Tunisia's foreign trade. By 1830 when France occupied Algeria, the Tunisian government and many of the country's citizens had accumulated considerable debts in France.

The Husainid beys had to wrestle with a variety of external problems. Algeria's Turkish rulers frequently meddled directly or indirectly in Tunisian affairs. In general, however, the beys not only checked Algerian ambitions in Tunisia but also played upon Tunisian resentment and fear of the Algerians to promote themselves as defenders of Tunisian interests. The dynasty walked a narrow line in its dealings with the Ottoman Empire. Subservience would compromise Husainid aspirations, but defiance could lead to the loss of the legitimacy provided by the Ottoman connection, as well as to added vulnerability to Europe. To establish a broad base of support providing the maneuverability and flexibility essential to a successful foreign policy, the Husainids cultivated links with the indigenous population in a way that earlier rulers had not.

The Husainids engineered and initially profited from the eighteenth-century integration of Tunisia into Mediterranean commercial circuits. As a result of this process, events in Europe affected the Tunisian economy more directly than ever before. Warfare on the continent, for example, allowed Tunisians to play a greater role in Mediterranean trade in the early 1800s. This commercial role, in turn, permitted their economy to recover from the disastrous effects of repeated inadequate harvests and epidemics. However, an important reason for Tunisia's inability to master the economic disorders of the 1820s was that they occurred at a time when the depressed international economy drove European businesspeople to pursue particularly aggressive tactics. Unable to compete with equal intensity, Tunisians saw the gap between their imports and exports widen and foreign merchants assume control of much of the country's international trade.

The ruling elite and bourgeois merchants of Tunis had monopolized the Mediterranean trade and were the first victims of its collapse. The increasing indebtedness of both groups to Europeans produced unsavory consequences. The beys attempted to compensate for their maritime losses by squeezing additional revenue from the interior, but the weakened rural economy doomed this approach to failure. Worse yet, it created ill will between the rural population and their urban rulers, weakening linkages traditionally crucial to the Husainids. By negotiating loans with European creditors or relying on European protection, the merchants placed themselves at the mercy of foreign interests. In a very real sense, international commerce provided the "Trojan Horse"[3] for the European political advance that characterized much of the nineteenth century and culminated in the French protectorate. After the French invasion of Algeria, however, Tunisian leaders made a last concerted effort at reform from within in the hope of forestalling a European takeover. Their troubles bought them only another half century of independence.

NOTES

1. Evidence in Lucette Valensi, "La Conjuncture agraire en Tunisie aux XVIIIè et XIXè siècles," in *Revue historique*, April-June 1970, p. 494, proves that there were only two satisfactory harvests in the first third of the nineteenth century, in 1824 and 1826.

2. These and other statistics bearing on the economic situation in Tunisia in the early nineteenth century appear in M. H. Chérif, "Expansion européenne et difficultés tunisiennes de 1815 à 1830," in *Annales Economies, Sociétés, Civilisations* 3, May-June 1970.

3. The phrase is used in Lucette Valensi, *Le Maghreb avant la prise d'Alger* (Paris, 1969). This introduction to North Africa in the early nineteenth century is available in English translation as *On the Eve of Colonialism: North Africa Before the French Conquest, 1790–1830* (New York: Africana, 1977).

6

Nineteenth–Century
Reform and Reaction

THE REIGN OF AHMAD BEY, 1837–1855

The French occupation of Algiers in 1830 heightened European interest in Tunisia. Soon after beginning the conquest of Algeria, France imposed a treaty on the bey banning the corsair activity that had revived during the Greek war, ending government monopolies, and guaranteeing Tunisian adherence to the earlier Franco-Ottoman Capitulations. By breaking the royal monopoly system, this accord opened Tunisian markets directly to foreign business interests. In the following decades, European consuls vigorously competed with each other in issuing threats and promises designed to force the Tunisian government to grant special privileges to their country's people engaged in international trade. The greatest victims of this scramble for commercial advantages were Tunisian merchants, who found themselves pushed farther than ever into the background of Mediterranean commerce.

In addition to their commercial clauses, the capitulations permitted all foreign consuls to settle legal disputes involving their nationals resident in the country. The consuls extended their judicial rights to include all cases in which the defendants were Europeans, although this interpretation had questionable validity. Many Tunisians saw advantages in linking themselves to Europeans: The wealthy could purchase foreign citizenship; others, by rendering various services, won for themselves the protection of the consuls. Both of these processes abused the spirit of the capitulations.

The number of Europeans in Tunisia multiplied rapidly. Most had some connection with commerce, although many Italian laborers and farmers crossed the Mediterranean to escape harsh economic conditions in their homeland. Political refugees from Italy added to

69

their numbers, and, until the 1930s, Italians formed the single largest foreign community in Tunisia. Many Europeans ingratiated themselves with the bey, joining his inner circle as advisors and, in some cases, officials of the government.

Tunisia's rulers understood the importance of balancing foreign interests and preventing any power from attaining dominance. Accordingly, they were alarmed in 1835 when Ottoman troops reoccupied the neighboring province of Tripolitania, which had enjoyed an autonomous status within the empire not very different from Tunisia's own. This Ottoman attempt to shore up the imperial position in the Maghrib was interpreted in Tunis as an indication that the Ottomans were preparing a similar fate for the Husainids.

By the same token, the completion of the French conquest of Constantine Province in 1837 disturbed the beylical government, in part because it had traditionally claimed areas of eastern Algeria, but more important because the victory brought the army of Tunisia's principal European creditor to its borders. To protect itself from these larger and more powerful neighbors, Tunisia turned to Great Britain. Committed to preserving the integrity of the Ottoman Empire and, by extension, to Tunisia's status as one of its provinces, Britain offered a barrier to French ambitions in the Maghrib without the need of an Ottoman offensive. France, however, naturally preferred an autonomous and, therefore, weaker Tunisia that it could manipulate without fear of provoking any controlling power. Thus the stage was set for the Anglo-French rivalry that continued until the eve of the French protectorate.

This complex situation awaited Ahmad Bey when he assumed the throne in 1837. He realized the urgency of defending Tunisian territory from foreign encroachment, but he also believed that too great a dependence on external forces would work to Tunisia's disadvantage. Consequently, the bey intensified a program pursued erratically by several of his predecessors, especially since 1830, of upgrading the Tunisian army and navy. He also knew that Muhammad Ali in Egypt and the Ottoman sultan Mahmud II had undertaken similar military modernization projects in the 1810s and 1820s with varying degrees of success. Ahmad's reforms included introducing modern weapons and equipment; hiring advisors from several European states to train his soldiers in the use of such equipment and to counsel his officers on matters of tactics and strategy; and creating a military training school at the Bardo Palace. Instruction at the school replaced the traditional training regimen of the bey's mamluks, and many of its graduates rose to important political and military positions. The small school could not, however, produce enough officers for the army. Throughout Ahmad's reign, the shortage of qualified leaders diminished the new army's effectiveness.

Foundries, textile mills, and other small factories designed to make Tunisia as self-sufficient as possible in military materiel were built during Ahmad's reign. The success of these tentative steps toward industrialization required royal support and patronage. Although Ahmad grasped the importance of an industrial base to support his armed forces, enterprises of this kind had none of the glamour and excitement of equipping his soldiers with modern weaponry, uniforms, and training. His frequent loss of interest in infant industries before they had had an opportunity to prove themselves doomed many to failure.

Ahmad's decision to conscript Tunisians for military service may have had more important long-term effects than any other change in the military structure. The random and disorganized recruitment system devised by the authorities did little to improve the army's fighting capabilities, but it did contribute to eroding rigid distinctions between state and society. By promoting the idea of a Tunisian homeland defended by its citizens, rather than by a handful of outsiders such as the janissaries or by only a few privileged tribes, the government attempted to instill in its subjects a greater sense of loyalty and of having a stake in the state's future.

Unfortunately, the financial burdens Ahmad's reforms imposed on many Tunisians offset the positive effects of this closer identity between rulers and ruled. The costs incurred in improving the military necessitated tax increases and led to the restoration of government monopolies on agricultural produce. These liabilities fell upon an economy already in dire straits because of the lack of exportable goods and the inability to compete with European products. When a confidant of the bey, General Ben Ayad, absconded with most of the national treasury in 1852, the economic situation seemed desperate. In the following year, Ahmad curtailed army expenditures to forestall bankruptcy. Even in these difficult circumstances, however, he insisted upon sending several thousand troops to the Crimean War. The bey sold personal valuables and contracted substantial debts to finance this venture, revealing the importance he attached to displaying Tunisia as a modern state worthy of treatment as an equal by the nations of Europe. The soldiers of the ill-fated Crimean expedition had no opportunity to prove themselves in combat, and their ranks were decimated by disease. Ahmad died before he learned of his army's failure to fulfill his expectations, and his successors paid scant attention to the military reforms that had occupied so much of his energy and revenues.

Tunisian participation in the Crimean War also allowed Ahmad to demonstrate his loyalty to the sultan. In the hope that better relations between the bey and the Ottoman Empire would facilitate its economic penetration of Tunisia, Great Britain tried to push Ahmad in this direction. Despite persistent urgings, however, the bey stead-fastly refused to apply in Tunisia the terms of various Ottoman reforms guaranteeing fundamental rights for all imperial subjects. Although not opposed to these concepts in principle, Ahmad believed that acknowledging them would cast him in the light of a simple Ottoman provincial governor. Throughout his reign, the bey took pains to demonstrate the progressive nature of his own administration and, therefore, the redundancy of the Ottoman decrees in Tunisia. His abolition of the slave trade in 1841 and the emancipation of slaves in 1846—both well in advance of such measures in the Ottoman Empire—were meant to convey an image of modernity. So also was Ahmad's imitation of European material culture, particularly following his state visit to the continent in 1846. His excessive expenditures for luxury items—graphically illustrated by the construction of a royal palace at Muhammadiyya that he envisioned as his Versailles—added to the drain on the treasury.

No clear-cut ideology dictated the bey's actions. They were instead the ad hoc defensive responses of an enlightened despot struggling to ensure his country's survival in the rapidly changing Mediterranean world. When traditional concepts proved inadequate for contemporary crises, Ahmad devised and imposed new, not always viable, methods. His reforms did not alter the basic structure of the state, nor did most of them entail significant social or economic change. They had little direct impact on the daily lives of most Tunisians, although there was widespread resentment over peasant conscription, the government's efforts to centralize power, and the lavish expenditures that inevitably led to higher taxes. On a more positive note, Ahmad's approach to Tunisia's difficulties thoroughly exposed its ruling elites to European ideals, suggesting to them potential benefits from the adaptation of such notions to their own society. In the final analysis, Ahmad's policy of grafting new institutions onto an essentially unchanged state system could not work. The next generation of Tunisian leaders would experiment with changes of a much more fundamental nature.

THE CONSTITUTIONAL EXPERIMENT, 1857–1864

European Economic and Political Influence

In 1856, Great Britain and France extracted from the Ottoman Empire a renewed commitment to liberalization as the price of their support in the Crimean War. Although ostensibly most concerned about the sultan's non-Muslim subjects, the European powers hoped that restraints on the arbitrary powers of the ruler and guarantees of basic rights and freedoms would also facilitate their own subjects' commercial ventures in the empire and the latter's integration into the international economy. Despite their earlier rivalry in Tunisia, Great Britain and France joined in pressing for similar reforms there. Some Tunisians, initiated to Western ways during Ahmad's reign, admitted the desirability of structural reforms designed to give the people evidence of the government's concern for their economic and political welfare. Such reforms, they believed, might engender a more stable and prosperous environment. But Ahmad's successor, Muhammad Bey (1855–1859), preferred to distance himself from the Europeans, with whom he thought Ahmad had consorted too freely, and their philosophies. He inclined toward retrenchment and conservatism. But European economic interests made it impossible for Muhammad Bey to survive in the shell into which he wished to retreat.

An incident in 1857 provided Great Britain and France with the excuse they needed to enter Tunisian affairs. Muhammad Bey had sanctioned the execution of a Tunisian Jew, Batto Sfez, for blaspheming Islam during an altercation. Expressing shock at the harsh sentence, the French consul pressed for the introduction of judicial reforms more clearly outlining the rights and duties of both ruler and ruled to prevent a recurrence of the Sfez incident. He also urged the bey to establish mixed courts to handle cases involving Europeans and to look favorably on European efforts to do business and acquire property in the country. How well Muhammad understood the implications of this final demand is apparent in his greater willingness to place restrictions on the religious courts by agreeing to some judicial reforms than to approve measures certain to result in increased European economic presence in Tunisia. But France rejected the bey's half measures. To prevent Tunisian noncompliance with the consul's suggestions from undermining French prestige, a fleet appeared in Tunisian waters to encourage Muhammad to act. With no illusions about his options, the bey issued the Ahd al-aman, or Security Covenant. It guaranteed civil and religious equality for all Tunisians—the superficial issue in the Sfez case—and promised new legal codes and mixed courts, both to protect the resident foreign community. As an assurance of the Europeans' freedom to engage in business and acquire property, the covenant also abolished the government monopolies.

The consular corps followed this success by extracting an agreement from the bey to grant a constitution based on the provisions of the Ahd al-aman. Muhammad had no enthusiasm for implementing this commitment, but he feared the consequences of continued great-power meddling. Reluctantly, the bey appointed several commissions composed of mamluks and ulama to draw up a constitutional document, the first of its kind in the Muslim world. Traditionally, Islamic states had regarded the Quran as the only constitutional document they required. Most ulama opposed the growing European influence epitomized by the pressure for a constitution. Their opposition stemmed not only from religious considerations but also from their strong links with urban merchants who had suffered from the European advance. In contrast, the mamluks were mostly veterans of the Ahmad Bey round of reforms. They realized the dangers of the European presence but were willing to take the risks involved, believing that only by forging an honest, efficient, modern state could Tunisia survive. The traditional Islamic viewpoint of the ulama inevitably clashed with their progressivism. The ulama, with little political experience, shied away from a process of which they did not approve, leaving the field open to those supporting reforms.

Muhammad's successor, Muhammad al-Sadiq Bey (1859–1882), formally promulgated the constitution in 1861. It established a constitutional monarchy with the bey's ministers responsible to the Grand Council, a newly created legislative body whose sixty members the ruler himself named. Muhammad al-Sadiq was more favorably disposed to the reform movement than his predecessor, seeing in it a means of attaining the sovereignty that the Ottoman Empire had always held back. He appointed to the Grand Council many people who advocated less arbitrary governmental procedures and the introduction of modern political and social concepts. These included the council's first president, a former mamluk of Ahmad Bey, Khair al-Din. But powerful vested interests, personified by the long-time prime minister, Mustafa Khaznadar, had benefited from the corrupt and venal practices of the past and now blocked virtually every important reform.

In fact, the power of Khaznadar and others like him had grown since 1857. Increasing numbers of European businesspeople, now more confident about their investments in a Tunisia that had legalized their participation in its economy, poured into the country. Naturally, they were anxious to establish contacts with Tunisians who had money to invest. They also sought to avail themselves of the services of people inside the beylical government with access to the corridors of power and a willingness, in return for financial considerations, to provide information and contacts that would facilitate their ventures.

Soon after the proclamation of the Ahd al-aman, Great Britain attempted to enhance its economic position in Tunisia and counterbalance French influence by creating the Anglo-Tunisian Bank to promote British investments. Prominent Tunisians, including Khaznadar, were given important positions with the bank, which quickly won a monopoly on the right to issue notes of legal tender. France opposed the beylical government's contacts with the bank and pressured the authorities to disavow them. Although Britain encouraged the bey to stand up to the French, the proximity of French troops in Algeria frightened him. After several years of wrangling, the Tunisian government dissociated itself from the arrangement, agreeing to pay an indemnity as partial compensation for British expenses.

Other European rivalries delayed or aborted useful development projects. Most foreign observers agreed that a railroad, which would promote agricultural development and natural resource exploitation, was essential for increasing trade. They further agreed on the importance of an early link between Tunis and its port, La Goulette. All prospective railway builders wanted similar concessions, differed little on the estimated cost of construction, and sought a partnership with the Tunisian government to guarantee their investment. The bey balked at the partnership arrangement, wisely rejecting a loan to cover his share of the costs negotiated for him by eager would-be partners in Paris and London. In 1863, after protracted discussions, British investors agreed to finance the railway on their own in return for permission to operate it for ninety-nine years. Their plan to extend the line from Tunis to the Algerian border met with vehement French objections. France resented both the influence that its commercial rival might derive from controlling the railway and the presence of a British venture on the very doorstep of French Algeria. The French consul successfully devoted himself to a campaign of sabotaging the scheme.

An 1858 British proposal to build a telegraph line, at no cost to the Tunisian government, connecting the capital with Europe via an already existing cable from La Calle in Algeria, produced a similar scenario. In this instance, however, the French consul compelled the bey not only to reject the British offer but also to accept a French one with much less generous terms requiring Tunisia to pay a portion of the project's costs. The insistence by French entrepreneurs that the bey engage them to construct an aqueduct to carry fresh water from Zaghouan to Tunis was another example of Tunisian dependence resulting in decisions contrary to the country's interests. Most knowledgeable Tunisians deemed the project too expensive and, more to the point, unnecessary. Nevertheless, well-placed bribes, wheedling, and threats secured a contract for the French entrepreneurs.

Shops in the market (*suq*) of the old quarter of Tunis. (Photo courtesy of Lewis B. Ware)

The expenses incurred by the beylical government's participation in such projects drained the treasury. Nevertheless, few voices from the inner circles of power spoke out. Those committed to equipping the country with a modern infrastructure and integrating it into the Mediterranean economy believed that European investment was imperative, whereas other officials regarded European involvement in the economy as a bonanza from which they derived enormous personal profits. The Zaghouan fiasco capped a series of extravagant and ill-considered expenditures that drove the beylical government into debt and forced it to seek foreign loans, further increasing outside influences. The Ahd al-aman and the constitution had restricted the bey's arbitrary tax-collecting powers at the very time that they had created an environment promoting the entry of foreign investors. In other words, they at the same time limited state income and heightened state expenses. In 1863, with its international debt standing at nearly 30 million francs, the Tunisian government succumbed to French pressures to conclude a loan with a Parisian banking firm. Although the loan was for 35 million francs, the government actually received only about 29 million after discounts and commissions were subtracted. The exorbitant interest rate of 12 percent translated into a payback of some 65 million francs. As a guarantee that it would not default on its annual payments of almost 7 million francs—an amount equal to roughly half the state's revenues—the government pledged its personal tax (*majba*) receipts. Since this levy rarely produced that much revenue, the bey doubled it, with disastrous consequences.

This tax increase was not the first financial burden to befall ordinary Tunisians because of the upsurge in European economic activity. As exports of wheat and olive oil mounted after 1857, domestic prices for these staples rose dramatically, triggering protests, including an 1861 march by angry citizens of Tunis on the beylical palace. Although economic issues lay at the root of these disturbances, the bey and his associates understood them as an expression of broader uneasiness over the magnitude of the European presence. Hoping to calm popular fears and lend legitimacy to the reforms and their results, the bey gave positions of responsibility to a few docile ulama willing to go along with his policies.

In addition to these economic concerns, the European wish to apply the reforms selectively also angered Tunisians. For example, Europeans continued to demand the tax exemptions and special judicial treatment they had enjoyed under the capitulations. They claimed all the benefits and protection of the constitution but accepted none of its obligations. The 1863 Anglo-Tunisian Convention was an effort to correct this situation. It placed British subjects in Tunisia on the same footing as Tunisians regarding taxes and legal matters, while according them the right to own property and conduct business without restrictions. The Tunisian government accepted this accord because it viewed British interests, unlike those of France, as essentially nonpolitical. Both the British and the bey hoped that by sanctioning a British economic presence in Tunisia, the treaty would deprive France of its predominance there.

Its more immediate effect, however, was to compound Tunisian irritation over the concessions and privileges extended to foreigners. The Ahd al-aman, the constitution, and the various development schemes had all been imposed on Tunisia from the outside. Lacking a base of broad support and popularly regarded as unnecessary, if not damaging, the reforms of the late 1850s and early 1860s had little chance of success. Anger over their costs, both monetary and psychological, erupted in a widespread uprising in 1864.

The 1864 Revolt

Ali ibn Ghdahem, a tribal leader, initiated the revolt in the regions of Kairouan and Le Kef. The tribespeople's complaints had a traditional ring to them and ostensibly focused on tax increases. Since Ahmad Bey's time, however, the central government had been continually attempting to strengthen its power in the more remote parts of the country. The tribespeople had always chafed at this process, but now they worried that the innovations of the reform era would further erode their independence. Of particular concern were possible alterations in the judicial system that would give the new courts powers formerly vested in the tribal chiefs.

The audacity of the tribes inspired some villagers in the Sahil to rebel; others took up arms under the duress of tribespeople who threatened to pillage their lands. For the first group, taxes again lay at the heart of the matter. The settled communities of the Sahil resented the assessment of the majba, which they had not paid before 1863. In addition to the detrimental effect of higher taxes on agriculture, the damage inflicted on small merchants and producers by the European takeover of commerce also provoked the Sahilians. Their adhesion to the revolt was a serious blow because as much as 50 percent of the state's revenues came from the Sahil, as did much of the army's human resources. Unpaid for almost a year, many soldiers refused mobilization orders at the time of the rebellion.

The tribal rebels believed that the bey still had the ability to correct their grievances, but the villagers, more attuned to political realities, understood that he had ceased to be a free agent. Their expectation that outside factors would determine the revolt's outcome prompted them to look to the Ottoman Empire for help. But France and Great Britain, both of which had dispatched fleets to protect their citizens' lives and property in Tunisia, were in far better positions to influence the outcome of events.

For the French, the reform movement they had helped set in motion in 1857 had turned sour. Instead of resulting in a Tunisia economically dependent on France, it had created an intensely competitive atmosphere inviting the involvement of France's European rivals. The revolt illustrated the depth of popular opposition to the reforms, as well as the likelihood that their continuation would cause further instability. France seized the opportunity afforded by the revolt. With its warships in Tunisian waters, France demanded that Muhammad al-Sadiq abolish the constitution. The bemused bey, whom the French had forced to introduce the document only a few years earlier, was now compelled by the French to rescind it.

In contrast, Great Britain wanted to keep the 1863 Anglo-Tunisian Convention intact to prevent total French domination of Tunisia. The British consul earned the gratitude of the bey by discouraging the rebels (in contrast to French officials who egged them on to convince the bey to accept their advice regarding the constitution). For example, he warned the Sahilians that the Ottoman Empire, over which his government exerted considerable influence, would not intervene on their behalf. On the contrary, the Ottomans gave the bey sorely needed funds to pay his troops. Many European businesspeople, anxious to restore order and proceed with their profitable enterprises, also lent the government substantial sums. In return, they took mortgages on future olive oil production, tightening the foreign grip on the economy.

Although the British helped to stifle the revolt, domestic realities also contributed to its containment. A government decision not to increase the majba came too late to mollify the rebels, but Prime Minister Khaznadar's divide-and-rule policy cleverly exploited tribal rivalries and weakened the opposition. Many tribespeople began to lose interest in the revolt as the harvest neared, and even Ali ibn Ghdahem appeared willing to give up the revolt in return for personal favors.

As summer 1864 wore on, the Sahil bourgeoisie gradually lost control of the revolt there as more radical popular leaders shouldered them aside. Middle-class fear of the mob, coupled with anxiety that the government might unleash the recently subdued tribes on their property, converted many former rebels into proponents of law and order and advocates of central authority. This divisiveness enabled the army to break the rebellion in the Sahil. Throughout fall and winter 1864-1865, a series of brutal sweeps by the army wreaked vengeance. The troops extorted money and agricultural goods from the Sahil to meet government expenses incurred in the fighting. Arbitrary levies forced many farmers either to sell their land or take out onerous loans. Often European businesspeople or Tunisians closely linked to them provided the loans or purchased the property. The army conscription of large numbers of Sahil peasants deprived the region of a considerable portion of its labor force, worsening the agricultural situation. Not surprisingly, a succession of inadequate harvests followed, underscoring the disastrous economic consequences of the revolt in the Sahil. The interior of the country fared no better. Government repression among the dissident tribes prompted many to flee into the desert or to follow Ali ibn Ghdahem in seeking refuge in Algeria. Ali slipped back into the country late in 1865 but was arrested and died in prison two years later.

The events of 1864 emphasized the tenuous nature of the reforms. The French role in eliminating the constitution demonstrated that European nations concerned with Tunisia would not support substantive reforms—even those of their own devising—if the conditions created by the reforms ultimately proved a liability to the interests of their own nationals. To the dismay of those in the elite who continued to believe that Tunisia's survival depended on such reforms, the revolt gave the bey an excuse to regress to the more authoritarian posture of earlier times. Governmental brutality and the impoverishment of large areas of the countryside spawned periodic uprisings for the next several years. They also drove a wedge between the royal family, whose junior members orchestrated some of the most vicious reprisals, and its subjects.

THE KHAIR AL-DIN ROUND OF REFORMS

Faced with an economy practically ruined in the rebellion and its aftermath, Prime Minister Khaznadar soon turned to his Parisian bankers for a second loan. Even so, state finances deteriorated rapidly. Despite the government's attempts to raise taxes, it could extract only limited funds from the beleaguered population. Meanwhile, it made no effort to curb its own extravagant expenditures. As early as 1866, interest payments on foreign debts were suspended, confirming the level of financial distress. At the end of the decade, Tunisia's European creditors formed an International Debt Commission to put the bey's fiscal house in order (and, of course, protect their own sizable investments) by setting aside a portion of Tunisia's annual income to retire the debt. The commission included representatives of the European powers, but its chairman was Khair al-Din, who had resigned from the presidency of the Grand Council in 1862 after quarreling with Khaznadar over the advisability of the first foreign loan. The Europeans, therefore, saw him as a symbol of fiscal responsibility.

The Debt Commission's opposition to concessions giving foreigners control of key facets of the Tunisian economy led to a new clash between Khair al-Din and Khaznadar. Like many in the bey's inner circle, the prime minister had grown wealthy brokering such deals. He now hoped to use British ambitions in Tunisia to maintain the influence that the Debt Commission sought to take from him. Toward that end, he secured lucrative concessions for British investors. Commissioners from France and Italy condemned their British counterparts and demanded Khaznadar's removal. Unwilling to risk a showdown with his creditors to defend Khaznadar's greed, the bey replaced him with Khair al-Din in 1873. The new prime minister had lived in Europe from 1862 until 1869, carefully observing its political systems and philosophies. He had set forth his own views on government in an 1867 essay entitled *The Surest Path to Knowledge Concerning the Condition of Countries* and now welcomed the chance to apply them in Tunisia.

During his four years in office, Khair al-Din made a valiant effort to avert a European takeover. He attempted to balance and hold at bay competing foreign interests while introducing domestic reforms aimed at achieving the order and stability conducive to prosperity. He admired the accomplishments of the European world, but Khair al-Din never abandoned the conviction, which separated him from many earlier reformers, that the wholesale importation of European concepts and institutions was inappropriate to an Islamic society with its own standards and traditions. He justified his actions in Islamic terms, often citing Muslim equivalents of European political and economic ideals. Consequently, his administration witnessed no restoration of the 1861 Constitution, which was so slavishly imitative of European models, but did include an effort to bring the ulama into the reform process. The bey's tyrannical behavior after the 1864 revolt, which did not spare the ulama who had supported the uprising, facilitated Khair al-Din's campaign to persuade the inherently conservative religious leadership of the need for changes guaranteeing the security of all Tunisians.

To Khair al-Din, the material success of the European states stemmed first from their citizens' confidence in their personal security and their belief that the state would accord them fair treatment. Khair al-Din intended to bring prosperity to Tunisia by building a strong but just state solicitous of its citizens' welfare and prepared to safeguard their lives and property against arbitrary actions. The prime minister began the process of restoring confidence in the government with a complete overhaul of the capricious tax structure. To eliminate corruption, he closely regulated the collection of personal taxes. He also ended the expensive but rarely remunerative mahallas to collect taxes from the more remote tribes. As an added incentive for economic revival, Khair al-Din canceled outstanding back taxes and granted tax exemptions to farmers who planted new olive and date groves. His decision to raise import duties and reduce export taxes allowed Tunisian merchants to compete more vigorously with Europeans.

Another means of increasing public faith in government was to staff the administration with people of high integrity and competence. Because many graduates of the Zaituna mosque-university customarily took up clerical positions in the bureaucracy, Khair al-Din urged reforms designed to render its traditional Islamic curriculum more appropriate to contemporary needs. But Khair al-Din also believed that government officials required a familiarity with other cultures, especially with that of Europe. Thus, he fostered the creation of Sadiqi College, a secondary school with a European curriculum, whose primary purpose was to train young Tunisians for state service.

Although anxious to promote Western knowledge, Khair al-Din remained a devout Muslim. As such, he saw merit in strengthening the connection between the bey and the sultan, thereby contributing to unifying a Muslim world beset by external pressures. He also hoped that a revival of the links between Tunis and Istanbul would tie the issue of Tunisia's international status to the broader "Eastern Question" and preclude a European takeover for at least as long as the empire lasted. This thinking naturally led Khair al-Din into a close relationship with Great Britain, which since 1830 had generally supported Ottoman claims in Tunisia. The once vigorous opponent of foreign concessions saw that the British received many attractive investment opportunities during his administration. He justified his actions on the grounds that British interests in Tunisia were economic only and provided a valuable counterweight to France's political ambitions. But British policy in the Mediterranean was gradually shifting away from a strong commitment to preserving Ottoman integrity. In the absence of strong support from London, most of the British projects collapsed. French and Italian interests leaped at the chance to reassert themselves. The futility of Khair al-Din's hopes of defending Tunisia by tightening its links with the Ottoman Empire became apparent in 1875 when the sultan requested Tunisian military assistance for his war against Russia.

The European powers found it awkward to oppose Khair al-Din's liberal reforms publicly, but they did not want Tunisia to effect an economic and political recovery that was so successful that it jeopardized their interests in the country. The prime minister's policy of playing the powers off against each other ended with all of them opposing him. The reformer had also made many Tunisian enemies, especially among those who had profited from earlier collaboration with the Europeans. Powerful figures like Khaznadar, who had been personally humiliated and financially hurt by Khair al-Din, bided their time, waiting for an opportunity to avenge themselves. Few of the ulama, whose support Khair al-Din had recognized as crucial to the success of his enterprise, understood or accepted the new ideas. His insistence on proceeding with the reforms thus led to an inevitable estrangement from the religious leadership. In 1877, the French consul, urged by Khair al-Din's Tunisian detractors, demanded that the bey remove him. Just as foreign intrigues had brought him to office, they now ensured his ouster and the demise of his reform program.

The 1878 Congress of Berlin, in which the European powers prevented a general war by acknowledging many of each other's territorial ambitions in the Ottoman Empire, sealed Tunisia's fate. Great Britain had recently acquired a controlling interest in the Suez

Canal Company, whetting its appetite for Ottoman territories in the eastern Mediterranean that could serve as outposts to protect the canal. No longer in a position to proclaim itself the watchdog of the empire's integrity, Great Britain offered Tunisia no protection at Berlin. Italian aspirations in North Africa had solidified since unification, and Italy put forward a claim on Tunisia based on its growing investments there and on the latter's substantial Italian population. French demands were even more vociferous, since the Franco-Prussian War had diverted French concerns early in the decade. At Berlin, Prussia encourged France to act in Tunisia, largely to distract public attention from the loss of Alsace and Lorraine and the need for revenge. Over the objections of Italy, which received a promise of support for its expansion into Tripolitania, the powers gave France a green light to enter Tunisia. Circumstances providing a sufficient excuse for intervention arose in less than three years.

Two groups competed for the political high ground in Tunisia during the half-century between 1830 and 1881. One, composed primarily of mamluks and members of the bureaucracy, advocated reform and westernization in the belief that the adaptation of European concepts and technology would enable Tunisia to better withstand the military, economic, and political pressures Europe was exerting. This group wanted neither to succumb to Western control of Tunisia nor to discard the country's Arabo-Islamic heritage, but its supporters knew that they could not achieve their goals without the cooperation and involvement of the West. Patriotism and idealism motivated some of the people in this camp; others were compelled by the personal profits made possible by contacts with European businesspeople and financiers. The second group, in which the bourgeoisie and the ulama figured prominently, feared that foreign influence would change Tunisia into a society with little room for them.

One important reason the reforms failed to restructure Tunisian society was that they were imposed from outside. The inspiration for the Ahd al-aman was European, not Tunisian, as was that for the 1861 Constitution. By accepting them, the bey compromised his autonomy. The first generation of reformers erred in relying on a foreign model requiring foreign support for its implementation. They hoped that the imitation of the West would bring stability and prosperity to Tunisia, in time turning it into an equal of the European powers. They failed to realize that the Europeans had no intention of treating Tunisia as a peer but preferred to keep the country in a subordinate role, taking whatever steps were necessary to thwart developments that might lead to a society capable of resisting the European will. Meaningful change, difficult enough to achieve in such circumstances, was made all the more elusive because so many Tunisians opposed the reforms, either in and of themselves or because of the incidental inconveniences, such as higher taxes, which accompanied them.

In the second round of reforms, Khair al-Din moved away from merely imitating European ideas, giving his program a more indigenous, Islamic flavor. Nevertheless, the Europeans' role in his rise and fall shows how easily outsiders could orchestrate events in Tunisia. Khair al-Din's ouster sealed the fate of the reform movement, ending any chance Tunisia had to develop the muscle to avert the ultimate outside orchestration that occurred a few years later when the beylical government was taken under French "protection."

7

The French Protectorate

Tribes living along the Algerian-Tunisian frontier generally ignored the boundary, both before and after the French occupation of
Algeria. French officials complained about the cross-border raids of
Tunisian Khrumir tribespeople, but they avoided provoking an incident
until 1881. A series of Khrumir raids in that year provided the pretext
for strengthening France's hand in Tunisia and thereby coming a step
closer to achieving the privileged position in the bey's domains
sanctioned for France by the Congress of Berlin. An expeditionary
force of 30,000 soldiers invaded Tunisia from Algeria, officially to
stabilize the borderlands. The French column met only sporadic
resistance and in less than three weeks reached the outskirts of Tunis.
The bey had little choice but to accede to French demands embodied
in the Treaty of the Bardo. The accord left the bey on the throne but
with considerably reduced powers. It permitted France to station
troops in Tunisia and prohibited the bey from dealing with other
foreign powers without French approval. To complete the strictures,
France named a resident-minister for Tunisia who was to act as the
bey's foreign minister, and the commander of the French troops took
charge of the Tunisian armed forces.

Significant opposition developed only in the interior of central
and southern Tunisia, where a full-scale revolt erupted during the
summer. Fear of the French was compounded by anger with the bey.
Tribal leaders chastised him for caving in to the French too readily
and questioned his fitness to rule. As they had in 1864, some rural
critics of the beylical regime made no secret of their hope for an
Ottoman restoration. There was far less sympathy for the revolt along
the coast. Urban leaders linked the well-being of their communities
to the maintenance of order, even preferring order imposed by the
French to tribal insurrection. The little support the rebels had in the
Sahil stemmed more from fear of reprisals than from shared con-

victions, as had been the case in 1864. Tunisia's rural hinterland and its coastal towns and villages looked at the world from quite different perspectives.

French and Tunisian troops overwhelmed the rural resistance, crushing it by the end of the year. Even discounting the military superiority of France, however, the revolt had little chance of success. Its most serious problem was leadership. The punishments inflicted on the tribes after the 1864 revolt had been so severe that some prominent local figures refrained from challenging Tunis a second time. For those who did take charge of the revolt, personal interest usually outweighed ideology. In most cases, their chief concern was to protect their land and their traditional prerogatives. Consequently, they often abandoned the field after receiving financial inducements or assurances of the preservation of their status.

With the rebellion collapsing, as many as 120,000 persons (10 percent of the total Tunisian population) sought to escape the clutches of the government by fleeing to Tripolitania. The bey realized that many of the refugees were locally important individuals whose followers would not readily accept others in positions of authority. Neither he nor his French mentors wanted a large number of disgruntled Tunisians beyond their reach in an adjacent country. With this in mind, the bey granted a general pardon, and most of the exiles returned within a year. The Ottoman authorities in Tripolitania, anxious to avoid French accusations that they harbored antibeylical elements, encouraged the Tunisians to return home. By 1885 virtually all of them had.

ORGANIZATION AND ADMINISTRATION

Those who stayed away until 1885 came back to a greatly changed Tunisia. Muhammad al-Sadiq Bey had died in 1882. His brother Ali had signed the La Marsa Convention in 1883. This document clarified France's role in Tunisia by formally establishing a protectorate. It also deprived the bey of control over internal matters by committing him to implement administrative, judicial, and financial reforms dictated by France. The responsibility for applying these reforms fell to Paul Cambon, who in 1882 had assumed the office of resident general, France's chief representative in Tunisia. Cambon carefully kept the appearance of Tunisian sovereignty while reshaping the administrative structure to give France complete control of the country and render the beylical government a hollow shell devoid of meaningful powers.

French officials used a variety of tactics to dominate the beylical government. They urged the bey to nominate members of the precolonial ruling elite to such key posts as prime minister because they knew that these people were personally loyal to the bey and would follow his lead in offering no resistance to the French. At the same time, the new rulers obtained the dismissal of Tunisians who had supported the 1881 rebellion or had otherwise opposed the extension of French influence. A Frenchman held the office of secretary general to the Tunisian government, created in 1883 to advise the prime minister and oversee and coordinate the work of the bureaucracy. French experts answerable only to the secretary general and the resident general managed and staffed those government offices, collectively called the Technical Services, which dealt with finances, public works, education, and agriculture. To help him implement the reforms alluded to in the La Marsa Convention, the resident general had the power to promulgate executive decrees, reducing the bey to little more than a figurehead.

France also left the framework of local government in place, while devising mechanisms to control it. *Qaids*, roughly corresponding to provincial governors, were the most important figures in local administration. At the outset of the protectorate, some sixty of them had the responsibility of maintaining order and collecting taxes in jurisdictions sometimes defined by tribal membership and sometimes by geographical limits. The central government appointed the qaids, usually choosing a person from a major family of the tribe or district to ensure respect and authority. Below the qaids were shaikhs, the leaders of tribes, villages, and town quarters. The central government also appointed them but on the recommendation of the qaids.

Most qaids and shaikhs grasped the futility of resisting the French, as well as the possibility of benefiting from collaboration with Tunisia's new rulers. Consequently, France allowed most of them to retain their posts. To keep a close watch on developments outside the capital, however, the resident general organized the *contrôleurs civils*. These French officials replicated, at the local level, the functions of the resident general, closely supervising the qaids and shaikhs. After 1884, a network of contrôleurs civils overlay the qaids' administrations throughout the country, except in the extreme south. There, because of the more hostile nature of the tribes and the tenuous hold of the central government, military officers, making up a Service des Renseignements (Intelligence Service), fulfilled this duty. Successive residents general, fearing the soldiers' tendency toward direct rule— which belied the official French myth that Tunisians continued to govern Tunisia—worked to bring the Service des Renseignements under their control, finally doing so at the end of the century.

Shoring up the debt-ridden and plundered Tunisian treasury stood high on Cambon's list of priorities. In 1884, France guaranteed the Tunisian debt, paving the way for the termination of the International Debt Commission's stranglehold on Tunisian finances. Responding to French pressure, the beylical government then lowered taxes, including the hated majba. French officials hoped that their careful monitoring of tax assessment and collection procedures would result in a more equitable system stimulating a revival in production and commerce and generating more revenues for the state.

To further consolidate French control, French law and French courts appeared as early as 1883. Since French law applied to all foreigners resident in Tunisia thereafter, the other European powers agreed to give up the consular courts they had maintained to protect their nationals from the Tunisian judiciary. The French courts also tried cases in which one litigant was Tunisian, the other European. The protectorate authorities made no attempt to alter Muslim religious courts in which judges, or qadis, trained in Islamic law heard relevant cases. A beylical court handling Tunisian criminal cases operated under French supervision in the capital. In 1896, similar courts were initiated in the provinces, again under the watchful eye of the French.

The protectorate also introduced new ideas in education. The French director of public education looked after all schools in Tunisia, including religious ones. Many colonial officials believed that modern education would lay the groundwork for harmonious Franco-Tunisian relations by providing a means of bridging the gap between Arabo-Islamic and European cultures. In a more pragmatic vein, schools teaching modern subjects in a European language would produce a cadre of Tunisians with the skills necessary to staff the growing government bureaucracy. Soon after the protectorate's establishment, the Directorate of Public Education set up a unitary school system for French and Tunisian pupils designed to draw the two peoples closer together. The French language was the medium of instruction in these Franco-Arab schools, and their curriculum imitated that of schools in metropolitan France. French-speaking students who attended them studied Arabic as a second language. Racial mixing rarely occurred in schools in the cities, in which various religious denominations continued to provide elementary schools. The Franco-Arab schools attained somewhat greater success in rural areas but never enrolled more than a fifth of Tunisia's eligible students. At the summit of the modern education system was Khair al-Din's Sadiqi College. Highly competitive examinations regulated admission to Sadiqi, but its graduates were almost assured government positions by virtue of their advanced training in modern subjects and in the increasingly important French language.

COLONIZATION

The protectorate set in place a framework conducive to increased European settlement in Tunisia. Nevertheless, colonization proceeded slowly at first, with the French authorities doing little to facilitate land purchases. During the 1870s, wealthy European speculators had begun paying handsome prices to Tunisian owners for rural property around the capital and in the Majarda Valley, along the railway line to Algeria. The same pattern continued in the early years of the protectorate. The absence of officially recognized deeds, combined with the practice of resolving property disputes in Islamic courts, left European buyers little security and limited their numbers to those financially able to absorb potentially considerable losses. The government introduced an optional land registration procedure in 1885, after which French courts heard disputes involving all registered property, regardless of the owner's nationality. But because property holders had to pay high fees for registration, the acreage recorded was minimal. A beylical decree of 1886 provided another source of land by permitting foreigners to acquire control over *habus* lands, not by purchase but through a system of perpetual rental. These estates, whose income was designated for either the support of religious and charitable foundations or individual family trusts, covered perhaps a quarter of the country.

The acquisition of land by Europeans did not necessarily mean the displacement of Tunisian peasants, nor did it usually bring about dramatic changes in crops or in traditional agricultural methods. Rather than evicting the Tunisians working on land they had purchased, most landlords made their profits by charging their tenants high rents, often forcing peasants into share-cropping arrangements. Even at the end of the first decade of the protectorate, only about 1,500 of the 10,000 French people in Tunisia lived in rural regions, and a very small number of these personally tilled the land.[1] In contrast, the more numerous Italians owned less land than the French but more often lived on it and worked it themselves.

Concern about the large Italian population prodded the protectorate government to lend official assistance to French colonization in the 1890s. In 1891, some state-owned lands were registered and parceled into small lots that the Directorate of Agriculture sold to the French at very low prices. When the directorate increased the size of these lots in 1896, buyers found them even more attractive, and demand rose. Partly in response to this surge of interest, France required the Habus Administration to set aside a minimum of some 5,000 acres annually for the Directorate of Agriculture to sell exclusively to French people, thereby freeing the latter from competing with Tunisians or other European buyers for choice habus lands. Speculators remained active, but these arrangements augmented the number of French settlers, or *colons*, on the land.

Another device to promote French settlement was the government's assumption in 1892 of most land registration fees. By making it easier for all land owners to legalize their claims, this decision produced disputes and tensions, particularly since Europeans and Tunisians frequently had very different concepts of property rights. From the French viewpoint, the security ensured by easy land registration enabled the colons to enter profitable but otherwise risky ventures. Olive growing rapidly came to dominate colon agricultural activity in the Sahil, especially around Sfax. Because olive trees required ten to twelve years to reach maturity, even wealthy investors hesitated to sink substantial capital into such enterprises without firm guarantees that their claim to the land would not be challenged later.

Colons enjoyed many other privileges. The protectorate government spent great sums to develop a transportation and communications network geared primarily to their needs. A vastly expanded road system, on which construction began soon after 1881, facilitated the movement of colon produce from farm to market. Railways linking Tunis with the Sahil and Bizerte with the Majarda Valley, both areas with large colon populations, supplemented the main line, completed in 1884, between Tunis and Algeria. Another railroad served the phosphate mines in the south. Improvements on the ports of Tunis, Bizerte, and Sfax during the 1890s benefited importers and exporters.

Protectorate fiscal policy also helped the colons. They did not, for example, pay the majba. Although all farmers theoretically paid the same taxes, those who utilized modern equipment—virtually all Europeans and almost no Tunisians—enjoyed an exemption from 90 percent of the taxes on cereals. No taxes were levied on grapes or products derived from them. Although some settlers (but few Tunisians) planted vineyards, viniculture never achieved the importance in Tunisia that it had in Algeria. With concessions such as these, the French authorities absolved the colons of all but minor assessments and placed the brunt of the tax burden on the Tunisians, who often accounted for as much as four-fifths of the protectorate's revenues. This allotment was made despite the impoverishment of many Tunisians, particularly the peasants, who could hardly comprehend the changes occurring in the countryside.

On the political front, the colons had access to the corridors of power. Their representatives participated in the deliberations of the Consultative Conference, an advisory body to the resident general set up in 1891. Since Tunisians won admission to the conference only in 1907, it long served as a vehicle for the expression and protection of colon interests.

As a result of these measures, French citizens owned 1.25 million acres in Tunisia by 1900, a fourfold increase since the start of the protectorate. By World War I, their estates encompassed 1.75 million acres, whereas all other Europeans in the country held a mere 300,000 acres. The total number of French inhabitants climbed steadily, but the Italians continued to outnumber the French until the interwar period. Even after a decade of strong official support for colonization, most French people still chose to reside in the cities. At the turn of the century, only about 12 percent of the French inhabitants farmed the land.

The economic impact of the colons belied their small numbers. By utilizing modern cultivation methods on the rich land the government helped them acquire, they produced a surplus of exportable wheat and olive oil. With imports declining slightly in the 1890s, colon farmers thus contributed to easing Tunisia's chronic trade deficit, although the cost of imports continued to exceed the value of exports. Colon enterprises were not strictly agricultural: They also built factories and mills, many for processing or packaging crops, and invested in the mining industry. But their hope that exports of Tunisia's substantial phosphate reserves—second only to those of the United States at the time—might correct the country's trade imbalance was shattered when the value of the mineral plummeted on the international market soon after extraction began in Tunisia early in the twentieth century. In the mines and factories of the protectorate, as in its fields, French people acted as managers, Italians or other Europeans provided skilled labor, and Tunisians were relegated to the most menial jobs at the bottom of the economic ladder.

To guarantee a market for the growing volume of Tunisian exports, France allowed goods from the protectorate duty-free entry after 1890. This first step toward integrating the Tunisian and French economies was followed by a similar accord in 1898 granting duty-free status to Tunisian imports originating in France.

Making the Tunisian market more accessible to French merchandise worsened an already serious situation. Long before the protectorate, European manufacturers had succeeded in imitating styles and designs used by Tunisian artisans in the production of a wide variety of goods. These mass-produced wares cost less and were more durable than those made locally by traditional methods. The lifting of import taxes invited a flood of such items into Tunisia. The demand for European articles was already on the rise, reflecting not only their lower prices and higher quality but also the desire of many upper- and middle-class urban Tunisians to emulate their Western neighbors. These were the very people who customarily patronized the artisans. The loss of their business compelled indigenous artisans to sell to a poorer clientele at necessarily lower prices. The concomitant loss of income reduced many artisans to penury.

TUNISIAN RESPONSES TO THE PROTECTORATE

The earliest pleas for changes in the system France had installed in Tunisia came from recipients of modern educations, especially Sadiqi graduates. They did not take an anti-French tack but rather urged France to honor the hitherto unfulfilled obligation, incurred with the assumption of the protectorate, to introduce reforms liberalizing the beylical government and enhancing its subjects' well-being. These people were intellectual heirs of Khair al-Din, convinced that their own society needed to make room for concepts and practices then current in the West but without discarding the Arabo-Islamic traditions on which it rested.

The precepts of the Salafiyya, or Islamic reform, movement very much influenced them. The proponents of this philosophy, the name for which was derived from the Arabic word for ancestors, asserted that modern Islamic society had deviated from its fundamental principles. Internal decay had resulted, making it easier for foreigners to dominate the Muslim world, as they so strikingly did in the late nineteenth century. A return to traditional ancestral values based on justice and equity therefore constituted an essential first step toward rejuvenating Islamic society and giving it the strength to withstand the enormous pressures of the modern world. Muhammad Abduh, perhaps the best known Salafiyya advocate, visited Tunis in 1885 and again in 1903. Realistically acknowledging that Tunisians could not through their own devices end the protectorate in the foreseeable future, he encouraged them to insist instead that France apply elementary reforms creating a fair and upright society.

In 1888, Salafiyya sympathizers in Tunis began publishing *al-Hadira*, a newspaper dedicated to promoting social change within an Islamic framework. Because the paper stressed the importance of adopting Western concepts, the French authorities viewed it as a potential bridge between the two communities and provided *al-Hadira* with a government subsidy, which continued until it ceased publication in 1910. The same coterie responsible for the paper established an educational organization, the Khalduniyya, in 1896, also with the blessing of Resident General René Millet. Named after the fourteenth-century Tunisian scholar Ibn Khaldun, it offered Arabic language instruction in a wide variety of modern subjects. Students at the Zaituna mosque-university were the prime targets of the Khalduniyya. Its founders envisioned the Khalduniyya as a vehicle for explaining the modern world, to which they had had considerable exposure, to those Tunisians less well acquainted with it. They also thought of themselves as the Tunisians best equipped to explain their society to the French.

The Young Tunisians, as the reformers called themselves, enunciated the views of only a handful of their compatriots, but their visibility garnered them opposition from several quarters. Few colons approved of their demands to make modern education more widely available to Tunisians. The French feared that such a policy would force them to compete with Tunisians who would qualify for jobs previously reserved for themselves. The equality implicit in such an arrangement was simply unacceptable to the colons, many of whom made use of political connections in Paris to lobby against any reforms. Under pressure from the colons and their Parisian friends, the Tunisian government closed a number of Franco-Arab schools, redirecting the emphasis to vocational training for Tunisians. Beyond the question of the kind of schooling Tunisians would receive lay the more critical one of their future status in the country. Deprived of the advantages of a modern education, they could never hope to attain positions of more than minimal influence or prestige in a polity dominated by Europeans.

The modernists were distraught at the colons' ability and willingness to badger the government into abandoning its supports for the rapprochement between the races that protectorate officials had long claimed to want and that the Young Tunisians continued to insist offered the best hope for progress in the country. To bring the plight of the Young Tunisians to the attention of a wider audience, perhaps attracting the support of more liberal French citizens in the process, a prominent reformer named Ali Bash Hamba started a French language newspaper, *Le Tunisien*, in 1907. *Le Tunisien* focused sharply on educational matters, but it took up other issues as well. Its editorials argued that Tunisians deserved a greater role in the management of their government, that Tunisians with modern educations were perfectly capable of holding important government posts, and that Tunisians were entitled to equal treatment with French people. *Le*

Tunisien never mentioned independence, and it stressed the concept of equity within the protectorate framework.

Bash Hamba and his associates on the staff of *Le Tunisien* paid less attention than their predecessors from *al-Hadira* and the Khalduniyya to Tunisia's Arabo-Islamic heritage. These men were not anti-Islamic, but they had accepted the notion of a limited sphere within society for religious activity. Their fascination with the West and their ideas about the role of religion in the modern world threatened and frightened the conservative ulama. The religious establishment especially resented criticisms of the Zaituna curriculum. The antagonism of the two groups peaked in 1910 when the Young Tunisians supported a student strike at Zaituna demanding the introduction of a more modern course of studies. Some alterations in the Zaituna curriculum had occurred after Abduh's visit in the 1880s, but the institution remained very conservative in the early twentieth century.

Eventually the protectorate administrators also soured on the Young Tunisians, whose militant pursuit of several causes alienated the authorities. Bash Hamba condemned the French plan to include Tunisia's highly Frenchified Jewish community in the French judicial system. He attacked this as a prelude to extending full French citizenship to Tunisian Jews, making them a privileged class in the protectorate. Two incidents in 1911 illustrated that the Young Tunisians were far from renouncing their interest in Islam, much to the regret of both the French and the ulama, who thereafter could no longer easily dismiss them as young radicals devoid of religious sentiment. The first was a campaign the Young Tunisians organized to send aid to Tripolitanian Muslims in the wake of the Italian invasion. The second was a riot at the Jellaz Cemetery in Tunis. Muslims feared that a city-ordered survey and registration would defile the burial grounds and ultimately lead to the expropriation of the land for other purposes. The authorities alleged but could never prove that the Young Tunisians had instigated the riot.

More likely, the turmoil had been spontaneous, and the Young Tunisians had capitalized on it. In any event, a highly charged atmosphere prevailed in the capital. The war in Tripolitania caused anti-Italian feelings to run high among Tunisians, whereas the Jellaz incident nurtured increased antipathy toward the French. When an Italian tram driver accidentally ran down a Tunisian child in 1912, the Young Tunisians organized a boycott of the trams, hoping to arouse support for their programs among ordinary Tunisians. The conditions for ending the boycott included the removal of Italian workers and, in keeping with Young Tunisian demands for equality, the promise that Tunisian tram workers would receive the same pay as their European colleagues for the same work. Protectorate officials worried about the implications of tolerating such open defiance of their authority, but the Young Tunisians refused to call off the boycott until their grievances were addressed. As a result, the government ordered the arrest of their leaders, many of whom were exiled, a ban on their publications, and the imposition of a state of emergency giving it special powers.

The Young Tunisian movement never recovered from this blow. Moreover, in the years leading up to World War I, the French and the traditional ulama drew closer together. This process had started earlier when the French had begun to realize that their sympathies with the Young Tunisians had aggravated the religious establishment. The ulama influenced far more people than did the reformers, whose appeal was largely limited to Tunisians with Western educations. France's disappointing recognition that the very class of westernized Tunisians on whom it had counted to legitimize the protectorate had become its most severe critics made closer relations with the ulama all but inevitable.

The French had no real liking for their new friends. They knew, however, that unless they shored up the traditionalists there was a very real danger that the Young Tunisians would broaden their appeal and grow strong enough to compel the ulama to cast their lot with them or lose credibility with the people, presenting France with a serious problem. By cultivating the ulama at this critical juncture, French officials short-circuited the formation of an anticolonial alliance between Western-educated advocates of social change and the traditional religious leadership—an alliance that did take shape in both Algeria and Morocco to the detriment of the French. An additional benefit in the timing of the French approach to the ulama was that it placed them squarely in the French camp by the outset of World War I, guaranteeing their loyalty, even in the face of calls from the Ottoman sultan for a jihad against the Allies.

NOTES

1. Estimates of the number of French farmers in Tunisia in the early 1890s are as low as thirty, a figure cited in Richard A. Macken, "The Indigenous Reaction to the French Protectorate in Tunisia, 1881–1900," unpublished Ph.D. dissertation, Princeton University, 1973, p. 303.

8

The Tunisian
Nationalist Movement

THE DUSTUR

World War I exposed Tunisians who had never before traveled beyond their towns or villages to the outside world. One hundred thousand Tunisians served in the French army or in work battalions manning the factories and mines of France. Forty thousand of them died or were wounded. Their experiences shaped their ideas about the proper future relationship between their societey and the West. The awe of French military might and the respect for European civilization that the protectorate had sought to instill in Tunisians diminished as they witnessed the enormous losses sustained by a French army grappling with the armies of other "civilized" Europeans. For the first time, it seemed possible that pressure might induce France to improve conditions in Tunisia. This hope rose further as they learned that not all French people looked on them with the same disparagement as did the colons. They encountered many individuals, especially leftists active in the labor movement, who sympathized with the plight of the colonized. Tunisian workers and soldiers were, therefore, reluctant to settle back into the social and political situation of the prewar era. They believed that their service in an hour of desperation obliged France to enact meaningful reforms in the protectorate structure endowing them with fundamental rights.

In search of a French commitment to apply to Tunisia the principle of self-determination included in President Woodrow Wilson's Fourteen Points, a delegation of former Young Tunisians traveled to Versailles in 1919 to meet with the peace commissioners. The group's failure to win concessions prompted one of its members, Abd al-Aziz Thaalbi, to write *La Tunisie Martyre*, a short book outlining a philosophy at odds with the Western sympathies of the prewar Young

Café in Tunis. (Photo courtesy of Lewis B. Ware)

Tunisians. Thaalbi, who had studied at Zaituna, had earlier worked
for Salafiyya-inspired reforms but had never agreed with the Western
proclivities of the more secular of the Young Tunisians. The central
thesis of his work was that Tunisia had enjoyed a golden age in the
nineteenth century, which the imposition of foreign rule had cut short.
As evidence of Tunisia's precolonial accomplishments, Thaalbi offered
the 1861 Constitution, which he urged the bey to restore. He rejected
Franco-Tunisian cooperation, arguing that the French presence had
brought only harm to the country. After a brief detention following
the publication of *La Tunisie Martyre*, Thaalbi assumed the leadership
of the newly created and still loosely organized Dustur (constitution)
party.

The Dustur coalesced around a nucleus of bourgeois merchants,
artisans, middle- and lower-level ulama, and community leaders, most
of them from Tunis. These were individuals whom the protectorate
had adversely affected, robbing them of the economic power and
political and social influence they had once enjoyed. Despite their
setbacks, they had never stopped thinking of themselves as the
backbone of Tunisian society—a narrow and unjustifiably self-centered
perspective. They had bridled at the Young Tunisians' claim to interpret
Tunisia for the French and were offended by the eagerness of the
Western educated, whom they scorned as social climbers, to assimilate
European concepts themselves and to urge their acceptance on others.
They had little sense of the realities of Tunisian life beyond the

boundaries of their own class. Their goal was not to spark a revolution but to find a mechanism to protect the few privileges remaining to them after nearly half a century of French rule and, perhaps in time, to restore others. Thus, the Dustur appears as a party unlikely to attract popular support. But the new attitudes fostered by the war and the fact that in the 1920s the Dustur was the only group prepared to question French policies in Tunisia converted it into a mass party in short order. Its leaders' prejudices, however, made it hard for them to appreciate the problems of other Tunisians or to take effective advantage of the unanticipated swelling of their ranks.

The Dustur program called for an elected assembly exercising real legislative powers; the formation of a government responsible to the assembly; elected municipal councils; equal pay for equal work; freedom of the press; and compulsory education for all Tunisians. In 1922, party leaders very nearly succeeded in a bid to strengthen their hand by enlisting the support of Nasir Bey. The ruler informed the French that he would abdicate if protectorate officials persisted in ignoring the demands of the Dustur but backed down when the residency made it clear it would not respond to threats.

This attempt to co-opt the bey cost the Dustur some support among potentially sympathetic French moderates, who interpreted the incident as a warning of future troublesome behavior. They found a second embryonic political party more to their liking. Hassan Qulati had founded the Parti Réformiste in 1921 with the intention of working with the protectorate government to achieve reforms, much in the tradition of the Young Tunisians. The backgrounds of the party's leaders differed very little from those of their Dusturian rivals, but their cooperative spirit attracted little popular support and the Parti Réformiste withered rapidly.

France did introduce some reforms in 1922, centering around the creation of a Grand Council with separate Tunisian and European sections. Reflecting the realities of power, if not of demography, the council's European members outnumbered their Tunisian counterparts. Colons elected most of the European representatives, but local advisory councils, organized at the same time and controlled by French officials or carefully selected Tunisians, appointed the Tunisian component of the Grand Council. Besides these obvious shortcomings, the council lacked meaningful legislative power.

The Dustur roundly rejected this system, which fell far short of its minimum goals. Parti Réformiste acceptance of the French package added nothing to its credibility in the eyes of most Tunisians. The feisty Nasir Bey had recently died, however, and his successor, Ahmad, had less enthusiasm for defending his nationalist subjects.

Fearing a repetition of the harsh measures taken to muzzle critics of French policies after the 1912 tram boycott, Thaalbi fled the country in 1923.

Although the anticipated repression did not materialize, opposition to the French during much of the rest of the 1920s came from labor organizations with ties to the party rather than from the party itself. The large number of European workers in Tunisia[1] had spawned the creation of a provincial branch of the Confédération Générale des Travailleurs (CGT), the main French labor union, in 1919. The CGT accepted Tunisian workers into its ranks, but, despite the common bond of wage labor, most CGT members took a typically condescending colon attitude towards the Tunisians. When European union members refused to support striking Tunisian dock workers' demands for equal pay for equal work in 1924, a major rift opened between the two groups.

The dockers turned to the Dustur for help. Its leaders saw the advantage of securing worker support, but few of them had any affinity with the Tunisian working class. They envisioned their role as one of direction of the workers, rather than solidarity with them. An exception was Muhammad Ali, a Tunisian who had worked with the Ottomans at the time of the Italian invasion of Tripolitania and had subsequently lived and studied in the Ottoman Empire and Germany. Under his guidance, the party had already begun to organize consumer cooperatives to enhance Tunisians' economic power. With Dustur support, Muhammad Ali formed the Confédération Générale des Travailleurs Tunisiens (CGTT) in 1924. Most Tunisian workers quickly deserted the CGT for the new union.

In addition to representing its members in collective bargaining, the CGTT provided instruction to improve workers' skills, continued setting up cooperatives, and undertook social welfare projects. But the critical issue of discrimination against Tunisian workers made it impossible, as it had been since the 1912 tram boycott, to separate socioeconomic concerns from political ones. The union's ties to the nationalist movement alienated many French leftists who, since the era of the Young Tunisians, had often sympathized with Tunisian attempts to improve their society. They tried to convince the CGTT, rather disingenuously in light of the attitudes of the CGT's European workers, that an emphasis on nationalist political issues created an artificial barrier impeding worker solidarity. Among the French, only the Communists supported Muhammad Ali.

From its founding, the protectorate authorities had tried to discredit the Dustur by suggesting a link (where none existed) between it and the Communist party. After 1924, Dusturian involvement with the CGTT and Communist interest in the union made it easy for the colons to project a guilt by association on the Dustur. When CGTT activists launched a wave of strikes in 1925, the French arrested Muhammad Ali and other union organizers, including many Communists. The Dustur had already begun to distance itself from the union in the hope that this would enable it to effect a deal with the socialist government in Paris. It now completely abandoned the CGTT to avoid being crushed along with it. Left in the lurch by French leftists and Tunisian nationalists alike, Muhammad Ali was deported and died in Egypt in 1928. Without his strong leadership, the CGTT collapsed. Even so, Dustur expectations of concessions from Paris came to naught. To restore calm in the protectorate, the resident general issued a series of decrees in 1926 restricting press freedoms and defining a broad range of political activity as criminal. The Dustur had little choice but to adopt a low profile.

The Dustur's dealings with the CGTT revealed several weaknesses in the party. They pointed up its leaders' difficulty in giving credence to the views and concerns of people with different backgrounds and outlooks from themselves. The people who headed the Dustur anticipated that independence would restore the power and privileges of which the protectorate had deprived them. For the workers, however, independence was the first step toward attaining the social justice in which few Dusturians exhibited much interest. The Dustur had never been comfortable with the mass support it had attracted. Despite the CGTT's efforts to rally Tunisian workers behind the Dustur leadership, class identifications kept the last from effectively capitalizing on this boon. Key party figures also displayed uneasiness with forms of protest other than the relatively mild methods of petition and supplication, reflecting an ideal of public restraint and moderation on which the Tunis bourgeoisie prided itself. Mass demonstrations, even if valuable, were vulgar and distasteful to these essentially conservative middle-class citizens. None had any desire to risk the humiliation of arrest by taking to the streets to lead the masses in protest.

In a more positive vein, the relationship between the Dustur and the CGTT, ambivalent as it was, nevertheless forced upon the party an awareness of social issues. Even if in the final analysis its leaders failed to deal with those issues effectively, worker demands for social and economic progress prevented the Dustur from becoming simply reactionary and nostalgic. Moreover, the CGTT-Dustur connection heightened the political consciousness of many Tunisians with little previous exposure to this sphere of activity. That many of them responded to issues primarily as Tunisians, rather than primarily as

·workers, indicated that, given a less parochial nationalist leadership, opposition to foreign control might take precedence over class identification, creating a formidable anticolonial movement. Finally, if the value of unionism as a nationalist weapon had been lost on many Dusturians, an emerging younger generation of nationalist leaders had clearly grasped its importance.

THE FOUNDING AND TRIUMPH OF THE NEO-DUSTUR

The Dustur hierarchy's inability to appreciate and accommodate popular sentiments proved to be the old guard's undoing as people with that talent made their presence felt in the Dustur ranks by the early 1930s. They had very different backgrounds from those of the party's founders and came from small towns and villages, often in the Sahil. Their success stemmed not from their manipulation of traditional powers and privileges attaching to middle-class families but from their access to modern education. Almost all had attended French schools, most were Sadiqi graduates, and many had gone on to obtain higher education in France itself. Familiar with contemporary political ideologies, especially those of the Left, they recognized the necessity of bringing the Tunisian people fully into the nationalist struggle. Perhaps even more important, their own backgrounds made them willing to take the steps necessary for achieving such an end.

Habib Bourguiba (Bu Ruqiba in its proper Arabic form), the dominant figure on the Tunisian political scene since the 1930s, epitomized this new generation. Born in 1903 in Monastir, a Sahil town, he studied at Sadiqi and earned a law degree in France, where he married a Frenchwoman. When he returned to his native country in 1928, he was distressed at how little progress the Dustur had made.

Unlike the leaders of the Dustur, Bourguiba and his well-educated peers did not reject the West. Neither did they accept the steady frenchification of their country, seeing it as part of a process leading to French assimilation of Tunisia. They chafed at their exclusion from the upper levels of the bureaucracy and resented efforts to increase the number of French citizens in Tunisia, both by promoting French colonization and by enacting legislation artificially enlarging the French population. Shortly after the war, the government bestowed automatic French citizenship on all Europeans born in Tunisia. This policy not only swelled the so-called French population, it also united Europeans of various ethnic backgrounds by erasing, at least in theory, distinctions between Europeans of French and non-French ancestry. Since 1923, Tunisians meeting certain educational and financial criteria had also been encouraged to adopt French citizenship. To do so, however, they had to renounce their right to trials in accordance with the precepts of Islamic law, which few Tunisian Muslims, even westernized ones, were prepared to do.

Such practices typified the protectorate's general disregard for Tunisians' feelings, but Bourguiba has singled out the Eucharistic Congress, held in Tunis in 1930, as the event most clearly symbolic to him of French arrogance. Tunisian Muslims took umbrage at this glorification on their soil of French Catholicism, which had not always dealt tolerantly with Tunisian Islam. Bourguiba concluded that the French were either oblivious to, or simply did not care about, Tunisian sensitivities. This intensified his fears for Tunisia's future and convinced him of the need to pursue a militantly anticolonial tack if the country were to be saved from absorption by France.

To disseminate their views as widely as possible, Bourguiba and his disenchanted associates within the Dustur founded the newspaper *L'Action Tunisienne* in 1932. Their handling of a controversial issue that came to a head that same year revealed their skill in mobilizing public opinion. A debate had arisen over the burial in Muslim cemeteries of Tunisians who had opted for French citizenship. Although Dustur strategists characteristically hesitated to enter the fray, the editors of *L'Action* vehemently asserted that naturalized Tunisians had forsaken Islam and could not be interred with the Muslim faithful. They labeled the senior ulama who had permitted the burials to proceed as docile servants of the French. At the same time, Bourguiba spoke out on the questions of traditional dress and the veiling of women, both customs quietly discouraged by the French. He defended these practices as aspects of Tunisian culture and criticized the French effort to eliminate them as part of the broader quest for assimilation.

Through this well-orchestrated press campaign the essentially secular Bourguiba established his credentials as a populist leader by promoting adhesion to the traditional Arabo-Islamic values most Tunisians cherished. *L'Action* made it perfectly clear that the country's religious and political leaders had done a better job of protecting their own status than of safeguarding the nation's heritage against encroachment. The popular resistance generated by Bourguiba forced the French to create separate cemeteries for the naturalized Tunisians. More important, the successful emergence of the *L'Action* group marked the beginning of the end for the old guard, foreshadowing the triumph of those Western-educated Tunisians bent on creating a state in which traditional values contributed to defining the national identity but in which the reactionary traditional leadership had little influence.

The protectorate government harbored no illusions about how dangerous the new generation of Dusturian activists was. When Bourguiba publicly called for Tunisian independence in 1933, the authorities immediately ordered the party dissolved. The offer of newly appointed Resident General Marcel Peyrouton to permit the revival of the Dustur a few months later, if it adopted a more conciliatory tone, split the nationalists. Bourguiba's unflinching opposition to any concessions led the party elders to expel him. In March 1934, he and other former members of the Dustur held a rump congress in the Sahil town of Ksar Hellal at which the Neo-Dustur party was born.

The very nature of the new party—its desire to appeal to the Tunisian masses and to use them to defy the French—guaranteed that it would not be tolerated. By late 1934, Bourguiba and most of the other top Neo-Dustur leaders had been arrested and sentenced to internal exile, usually in the Sahara. In the months immediately after the Ksar Hellal Congress, however, Bourguiba and his colleagues had devoted their attention to structuring the Neo-Dustur into tightly knit cells, a technique they borrowed from the Communists and one that allowed the party to continue functioning without its leaders. Consequently, the French decapitation of the Neo-Duster failed to destroy it. Indeed, it proved a tactical blunder enhancing the public image of the party and that of its imprisoned organizers. Neo-Dustur militants, backed by former supporters of the CGTT, mounted demonstrations during 1935 and 1936, eventually forcing the recall of the hated Peyrouton.

Tunisia's Troubled Economy

Tunisia's economic situation contributed significantly to the rise and growth of the new party. The Dustur's failure to manifest any real concern for the hardships of Tunisian farmers in the 1920s and 1930s helps explain the rural enthusiasm for the more outspoken Neo-Dusturians, who did take an interest in agricultural matters. Colon farmers had experienced an era of prosperity in the postwar years. As part of its policy to expand the French population of the protectorate, the government made easy credit available to prospective settlers and further modified customs arrangements to facilitate the sale of Tunisian farm products to France.

But Tunisian peasants suffered as an increasing number of French settlers directly worked an increasing proportion of the land.[2] Europeans owned roughly a fifth of all cultivated land in the protectorate by the late 1930s, a figure that held steady until independence. The high price and steady demand for wheat on the readily accessible

French market made it the primary crop of colon farmers who derived the maximum benefit from their land by adopting capital-intensive agricultural techniques. As a result, many Tunisian renters and tenant farmers lost their access to land, forcing them to choose between day labor; the exploitation of marginal tracts ignored by the Europeans; or migration to the cities to join other dispossessed rural families in the slums and *bidonvilles* (shanty towns) springing up there. The pursuit of high profits also led the colons to sow uncultivated lands previously used for pasturage, endangering the livestock on which many Tunisians depended for their livelihood. Finally, the colons' heavy use of fertilizers exhausted the soil much more rapidly than did traditional cultivation methods.

The worldwide depression of the 1930s hit Tunisia hard. The market value of its most important products (wheat, olive oil, wine), which had begun to decline as early as 1926, reached an all-time low in 1934. To avert the total ruin of the export-dependent colon farmers, the government imposed a debt moratorium in 1934 and intervened to stabilize the price of wheat, their major export. French quotas on imported wines hurt the owners of Tunisian vineyards, who were almost exclusively colons. In another attempt to shore up colon agricultural interests, the government financed the massive uprooting of grape vines and their replacement with fruit trees, which it was hoped would be more profitable. The price of olive oil fell drastically as the produce of new trees, planted in the postwar boom, flooded the market. The prospects for alleviating the colons' plight improved after 1936, as the Spanish Civil War and the League of Nations sanctions on Italy reduced the agricultural exports of these two competitors of Tunisia, opening wider markets for the protectorate's produce.

These European events had little impact on Tunisian farmers because few exported their crops, and government aid programs during the depression did not benefit them very much because most programs were tailored to assist the larger colon producers. The debt moratorium had helped to some extent, but for most peasants it merely postponed the day of reckoning on obligations they could not have met in the best of circumstances. Those in the most dire straits lacked the land needed as collateral to obtain low-interest government loans. For a large number of rural Tunisians, the depression simply meant impoverishment. Olive producers were among the most seriously affected. Because their trees required intensive care, most producers in the traditional sector tended small plots with only a thin margin for survival.

In sum, the resources available to rural Tunisians eroded steadily in the 1920s and 1930s. Colon land acquisitions and the growth of mechanized agriculture resulted in the overpopulation of the traditional rural sector by the time the depression struck. Ironically, French successes in improving health care and upgrading sanitary conditions also contributed to rural overpopulation and to the socioeconomic problems attendant on it. The destructiveness of the interwar agrarian crisis added immeasurably to the initial attractiveness of the Neo-Dustur to rural Tunisians. The Sahil origins of so many of the party's early leaders also strengthened its appeal to those nonurban segments of the population whose backing the Neo-Dustur needed to build a mass base.

The Collapse of the Popular Front and Renewed Violence

If the year 1936 raised settler hopes for an end to their economic dilemma, it raised Tunisian hopes for progress on the political front. French elections brought to power the left wing Popular Front coalition, which soon ordered the release of the Neo-Dustur political prisoners. Bourguiba and his associates, well aware of the philosophies of the Popular Front politicians, believed that they would join in a search for mutually acceptable solutions to the most pressing Neo-Dustur grievances.

With the ban on political activity lifted, Bourguiba again used the pages of *L'Action* to publicize his views. Independence remained his first priority, although he acknowledged the desirability of some form of ongoing association with France. The agricultural calamities of the post–World War I era—and the growing rural popularity of the Neo-Dustur—prompted demands for the cessation of official support for colonization. *L'Action* also called for the formulation of a constitution (but not the restoration of the 1861 organic law) and a greater role for Tunisians in the political process.

The Popular Front government collapsed after only fifteen months, without having instituted any reforms in the protectorate. Bourguiba had overestimated the political capabilities of the French liberals and underestimated the obstructionist tendencies of the French Right. The Popular Front did sympathize with the problems of the colonized, but it had to devote a disproportionate amount of its attention to keeping itself in office, leaving little time for overseas issues. Moreover, the colons marshaled their forces to lobby against any changes in the status quo capable of threatening their investments, which were beginning to show signs of recovering from the depression. Finally, the French military opposed concessions to nationalists anywhere in

North Africa. Foreseeing a continental war on the horizon, French general officers warned the Popular Front not to jeopardize their access to the Maghrib and its human and material resources.

The failure to advance their cause, even with the relatively congenial Popular Front in office, set in motion the radicalization of the Neo-Dustur leaders. The attempt by Abd al-Aziz Thaalbi, who returned to Tunisia in 1937, to regain control of the nationalist movement furthered this process. The country had changed greatly during the fourteen years of Thaalbi's absence. His emphasis on traditional Arabo-Islamic values, always at the heart of the Dustur philosophy, clashed with the more modern, more secular, and by 1937 far more popular, views espoused by the Neo-Dustur. For a brief time, the two generations of nationalist leaders cooperated uneasily, but neither was willing to recognize the preeminence of the other. Realizing that Thaalbi would not step aside of his own accord, the Neo-Dustur undertook a campaign of harassment, hoping to persuade him to give way to Bourguiba. Party militants' practice of interrupting his speeches forced Thaalbi into the awkward position of requiring police protection when he appeared in public. Nothing could have illustrated the bankruptcy of the Dustur more clearly. As if to prove to both the French and Thaalbi the Neo-Dustur's right to the nationalist leadership, Bourguiba organized and led a series of mass demonstrations of the kind Thaalbi never could nor would.

As in 1933, French hints of reforms in return for moderation split the nationalists. Pointing out the harsh treatment France was meting out to Algerian and Moroccan opponents of colonialism, Bourguiba expressed doubts about French sincerity. He argued that French overtures were merely attempts to divide the movement and that only when a popular struggle had left them with no choice would the French accede to nationalist demands. Not all Neo-Dusturians accepted this hard line. Many who advocated more moderate tactics, including Mahmud Matari, a long-time party member and the Neo-Dustur's president, resigned, but Bourguiba would not be swayed.

Violence erupted in Tunis in April 1938. Police efforts to contain a crowd of Neo-Dustur supporters protesting the arrest of a party organizer sparked a riot that took more than a hundred lives. After arresting Bourguiba and other leaders, the authorities banned the Neo-Dustur. Its cellular structure, which had served Bourguiba well in mobilizing demonstrators and maintaining discipline among them, now once again enabled the party to survive a period of repression. At the outbreak of World War II, Bourguiba and his colleagues remained in prison in France, still awaiting trial.

TUNISIA IN WORLD WAR II

The war presented Tunisian nationalists with the possibility of forging an alliance with the Axis powers to defeat their common French enemy. Despite his commitment to terminate the French protectorate, the pragmatic Bourguiba had no desire to exchange the control of republican France for that of Fascist Italy or Nazi Germany, whose ideologies he abhorred.[3] Flawed as French behavior in Tunisia had been, he preferred his French adversaries to Hitler or Mussolini and feared that associating with them might bring to the nationalist movement a short-term triumph but result in a long-term tragedy. Like most Tunisians, Bourguiba particularly suspected the Italians of harboring designs on the country, especially after Mussolini's denunciation of the French protectorate in 1938.

Following the fall of France, administrators representing the German puppet government in Vichy received a reasonably good reception in the protectorate. On the whole, Tunisians regarded rule from Vichy as more desirable than the extension of Italian influence from neighboring Libya, and many colons sympathized with the new government's right-wing policies. Despite Bourguiba's protestations of loyalty, his advice to his fellow Tunisians to remain faithful to France, and his refusal to collaborate with his jailers, Neo-Dustur demonstrations not only failed to persuade Vichy to release him but occasioned the arrest of additional party members in 1940 and 1941.

With the Neo-Dustur leaderless, Munsif Bey, who came to the throne in 1942, attempted to take charge of the nationalist movement himself. He requested that France enact a series of reforms allowing Tunisian representation in the government, requiring equal pay for equal work, and providing compulsory education in Arabic. Munsif no doubt knew that an alliance between the French-protected ruler of Morocco, Sultan Muhammad V, and the Istiqlal (Independence) party, had been advantageous for both the palace and the nationalists. He planned to use the prestige of the royal family and the popularity he hoped to gain by focusing more closely on his subjects' concerns than had his predecessors, to push France toward altering Tunisia's political status. The Neo-Dustur directors still in the country could hardly compete with the monarch and made no effort to stand in his way. Munsif's plans were short-circuited, however, as the war impinged more directly on Tunisia.

An Allied task force landed British and U.S. troops near Casablanca, Oran, and Algiers in November 1942. Operation Torch, the first Allied offensive in the war against the Axis powers, quickly resulted in the occupation of Morocco and Algeria, but its ultimate objective was Tunisia, which the Allied commanders planned to use as a jumping off point for an invasion of Italy. In response to the Allied incursions, Germany immediately seized Tunisia and poured troops and supplies into the country. Nevertheless, British forces entered western Tunisia and began to advance into the Majarda Valley before the end of the year.

In the same month as the Torch landings, Field-Marshal Bernard Montgomery defeated General Erwin Rommel at the Battle of al-Alamain in Egypt and pursued the retreating Axis troops westward across Libya. The Allied strategy called for the Torch forces to move east and for Montgomery to push Rommel's army north along the Tunisian coast, ultimately squeezing the Germans and Italians between them.

U.S. units with no combat experience held the southern sector of the front established by the Allies as they advanced into Tunisia. They bore the brunt of a major Axis attack in February 1943. Rommel broke through the Kasserine Pass and threatened to encircle the Allies until a quick counterattack stalled his drive. In late March, Montgomery smashed the German defenses along the Mediterranean, linked up with the U.S. troops, and started north. British and U.S. soldiers in the Majarda Valley, however, continued to encounter strong German resistance. Only after bitter combat to the west of the city did they enter Tunis on May 7, 1943. Meanwhile, the Allied vise tightened around the Axis armies, trapping them on the Cape Bon peninsula. Some Germans and Italians managed to escape by sea, but the Allies took a quarter of a million prisoners. Fighting ended throughout Tunisia on May 12, 1943.

THE TERMINATION OF THE PROTECTORATE

The Reassertion of Neo-Dustur Leadership

On the political front, Admiral Jean Esteva, the Vichy resident general, had released many Neo-Dustur prisoners in the interval between the Torch landings and the German occupation of the country. His actions did not so much represent a change of heart about the nationalists as a fear that the Germans would free Tunisian political prisoners in the hope of creating both pro-German and anti-French sentiments among them. Esteva's concern stemmed in part from the Nazis' decision to release Bourguiba when they moved into unoccupied France following Operation Torch. After a brief stay in Rome, Bourguiba returned to Tunis in April 1943.

During the occupation, Munsif Bey maintained correct but not cordial relations with the German authorities, using the unstable political situation to embellish his own position. Toward the end of 1942, he formed a ministry omitting several traditional posts without Admiral Esteva's approval. Munsif probably viewed this step as a prelude to more serious future reforms. The reviving Neo-Dustur took its cue from the bey and resumed its campaign for independence. But the liberation of Tunis changed Munsif's fortunes for the worse. When the Free French assumed control of the protectorate, they falsely accused Munsif of collaborating with Germany and compelled him to abdicate. This no-nonsense policy clearly signaled France's intention of fully reestablishing its grip on Tunisia.

Munsif's deposition once again left the Neo-Dustur as the main outlet for the expression of nationalist sentiments. Despite France's hard-line approach to the bey, Bourguiba believed that the Axis defeat in North Africa presented an opportunity for Franco-Tunisian cooperation in reforming the protectorate. As Bourguiba had advocated since 1939, Tunisians had not aided the Fascists or otherwise obstructed France's war efforts. He now sought a reciprocal gesture from France in the form of a loosening of political strictures. But the French made no such gesture and, in fact, took steps after the liberation to strengthen their control over the beylical government.

The death of Abd al-Aziz Thaalbi in 1944 made it easier for Tunisians who differed on how to deal with the protectorate authorities to cooperate. Disturbed by the unyielding attitude of France, Neo-Dustur, Dustur, and Communist leaders, supporters of Munsif Bey, labor activists, educators, and religious officials all joined in 1944 to issue the "Manifesto of the Tunisian Front" calling for self-government and an elected assembly but, owing to the diverse views of its authors, cautiously omitting any demand for independence. To mobilize public opinion, the Neo-Dustur began to organize interest groups based on such clearly identifiable segments of the population as students, farmers, and women. During 1944 and 1945, Farhat Hashid, a veteran labor organizer, was at work laying the groundwork for another important interest group, the Union Générale des Travailleurs Tunisiens (UGTT). Hashid shared many of the Neo-Dustur's objectives, and the UGTT and the party provided each other with assistance and support.

When France responded to the nationalists' demands in 1945 with only minimal compromises, Bourguiba concluded that Paris would not of its own accord go beyond insignificant concessions. Faced with a choice between promoting violence inside the country or attempting to generate enough external support to pressure France into reconsidering its Tunisian policies, Bourguiba opted for the latter course. He left the country in April 1945, going first to Cairo to lobby at the newly created Arab League. For the next four years, Bourguiba traveled throughout the Middle East, as well as in the United States, where influential labor organizations sympathized with the Neo-Dustur because of the nationalists' links with trade unionism. In 1948, Bourguiba helped found the Committee for the Liberation of the Arab Maghrib, an agency headquartered in Cairo that coordinated contacts among nationalist leaders from all of France's North African possessions. The concentration of the Arab world on Palestine in the postwar years, however, made it difficult for the North Africans to command very much attention from their fellow Arabs.

In Tunisia itself, tension mounted during Bourguiba's absence. French intransigence precipitated a rash of UGTT-sponsored strikes and other political demonstrations throughout 1946. At a rally in the summer of that year, Salah Ben Yusuf, secretary general of the Neo-Dustur, expressed the frustration and anger of growing numbers of politically conscious Tunisians. His assertion of Tunisia's right to immediate and unrestricted independence won the backing of almost all nationalists, including the remnants of the Dustur. In the past, Bourguiba had always couched his references to independence within a vague future framework. The immediacy of Ben Yusuf's demand represented a new departure for the Neo-Dustur and, more important, foreshadowed a split in party ranks between moderates and radicals. Hoping to aggravate the strains within the nationalist movement, the protectorate authorities invited Bourguiba to return to Tunisia in 1949. Well aware of Ben Yusuf's growing influence and unable to do more to raise international support, Bourguiba welcomed this opportunity and resumed his role as party leader. In keeping with the prevailing atmosphere within the Neo-Dustur, he lost no time in pressing France to move toward the goal of an independent Tunisia, although he continued to advocate a gradualist approach.

From Cosovereignty to Independence

The French recognized the growing vigor of the opposition but remained unwilling to accept the notion of independence. Instead, they searched for a formula of "cosovereignty" that would satisfy the Tunisians without entirely relinquishing French control. Promises that a new ministry formed in 1950 would explore prospects for internal autonomy led to the Neo-Dustur's first participation in a Tunisian government. Ben Yusuf accepted a ministerial portfolio, whereas several other members of the government were party sympathizers. Measures approved by the government in the following year limited the powers of both the resident general and the secretary general, while guaranteeing a percentage of positions for Tunisians at various levels of state service.

Although the Neo-Dustur gained official recognition in August 1951, the party showed no signs of subservience. Bourguiba took the view that the concept of cosovereignty fell short of Tunisian aspirations. He insisted upon a completely Tunisian government; an assembly reflecting demographic realities and not unfairly weighted to protect European interests, as all previous experiments at a legislative body had been; and the more rapid incorporation of Tunisians into the bureaucracy. He forcefully rejected a French proposal for municipal elections in which colons would vote but at the same time tried to assure the French that a nationalist government would not ignore their legitimate concerns.

Bourguiba's protestations did not sway the colons. More unified than ever before, they had formed their own party, the Rassamblement française de Tunisie, to guard against any additional changes in the status quo. The vehemence of their protests undermined the continuation of the 1951 reform efforts, which might otherwise have found some middle ground between the French and the nationalists, particularly since France was moving in such a direction. In addition to the mounting domestic popularity of the Neo-Dustur, France could not indefinitely ignore international pressures for decolonization in the postwar era. Bourguiba tried to capitalize on this situation by again traveling abroad as a spokesman for Tunisian nationalism. Neo-Dustur attempts to internationalize the Franco-Tunisian dispute culminated when Ben Yusuf went to the January 1952 meeting of the UN Security Council in Paris to place Tunisian grievances before the world body.

This overture coincided with the appointment of Jean de Hautecloque as resident general. Because the French government unconditionally rejected outside intervention in protectorate affairs, de Hautecloque instructed Amin Bey to demand the resignation of the prime minister who had authorized Ben Yusuf's mission and to recall Ben Yusuf himself. When the bey refused, de Hautecloque ordered the arrests of Bourguiba and most other important Neo-Dustur officials in the country. Bloody riots ensued, checked only by the imposition of a state of emergency. Under great duress, the bey dismissed the government and grudgingly appointed a new prime minister wholly lacking in popular support. Any prospects for a revival of talks ended with the assassination of Farhat Hashid by colon terrorists later that year.

After permitting the crisis to smolder through 1953, France, now represented by Resident General Pierre Voizard, took a new tack. Voizard began his tenure in 1954 by releasing many political activists, although Bourguiba remained in prison. He then initiated discussions with a group of Tunisian interlocutors, none of whom were affiliated with the Neo-Dustur, rather wistfully hoping that the exclusion of the most outspoken nationalists would facilitate the search for an acceptable political arrangement. Voizard's approach did lead to new reforms, but they proved unworkable. The Neo-Dustur, which was easily able to galvanize the opposition, rejected them as half measures. Ironically, the colons also rejected them, asserting that they included too many concessions to the Tunisians. More serious than Voizard's failure to find Tunisians willing to collaborate and capable of bringing public opinion along with them was the reaction of the mainstream nationalists. For the first time, their frustrations boiled over into armed resistance. Street fighting erupted in urban areas, and bands of *fallaqa* (literally, bandits) roamed the countryside attacking French farms and police stations.

French Prime Minister Pierre Mendès-France keenly appreciated the gravity of the Tunisian situation. Having already vowed to end the painful and costly colonial war France had been fighting in Indo-China, he had little enthusiasm for embarking on a prolonged campaign in Tunisia, where some 70,000 French troops were already engaged in combating the fallaqa. The prime minister decided that granting internal autonomy offered the best prospects of bringing the situation in Tunisia under control. Talks began in summer 1954 but proceeded slowly, with France seeking to retain as much influence as possible and the fallaqa intensifying their activity whenever French negotiators appeared to drag their feet. Real progress came only in 1955, when the French released Bourguiba and allowed him to take charge of the Tunisian negotiating team. An accord was reached in April, and Bourguiba returned to Tunisia in triumph the following month.

Bourguiba and the French, however, viewed the new arrangement in entirely different lights. For the latter, internal autonomy was an end in itself; for Bourguiba it was a stepping stone toward complete independence. The pragmatic Tunisian recognized that Mendès-France could not, for a variety of reasons (key among them the threat of domestic opposition to such a policy triggering the collapse of his government), promise more than internal autonomy but that he was willing to pledge himself to that proposition. Bourguiba seized the proffered half-loaf rather than futilely insisting on what France had no intention of providing at that moment. His plan—to utilize what he could attain as a basis for securing additional future gains—

illustrated the essence of the political philosophy called Bourguibism. The Neo-Dustur leader skillfully combined an inflexibility of ultimate principles with great flexibility in determining what tactics would best achieve them. Gradualism and compromise also characterized Bourguiba, as each small gain was added to earlier ones in building toward the final goal.

The more radical of Bourguiba's associates, led by Ben Yusuf, objected to his gradualist approach and accused him of submissiveness. The frequency and bitterness of their charges increased as the first government formed under the internal autonomy accords (in which several prominent Neo-Dusturians, but not Bourguiba, headed ministries) focused on stabilizing the country rather than immediately pressuring the French for more concessions.

At the Neo-Dustur Congress in October 1955, Ben Yusuf, with the backing of a fledgling group of Tunisian pan-Arabists, openly challenged Bourguiba's policies and leadership. He and his supporters advocated pursuing anticolonialism to its logical conclusion. They condemned Bourguiba's moderation, which, they believed, produced only inconclusive results, especially when compared with the achievements of the more extreme leaders of the Egyptian and Algerian revolutions. Much to Bourguiba's distress, they also argued for subordinating programs of social change to the campaign to gain independence not only for Tunisia but also for other Arab states still under colonial rule. Bourguiba, in contrast, believed that such a course of action would not only delay independence but would make its acquisition far more costly in terms of human lives. The emotional appeal of pan-Arabism helped Ben Yusuf to generate broad support, but in a showdown vote of party delegates Bourguiba's position prevailed. Fearful of his rival's popularity, Bourguiba engineered his expulsion from the Neo-Dustur. Ben Yusuf left the country shortly thereafter but continued his political diatribe against Bourguiba from abroad.

The apparent quieting of the Tunisian crisis gave France only slight consolation. Full-scale rebellion had erupted in Algeria in November 1954, while Moroccan nationalists were steadily gaining ground in their struggle against the protectorate. Algeria was, and always had been, the centerpiece of French North Africa—so much so that its status was not that of a colony but of a French *département* (a political subdivision). After the defeat in Indo-China, and with calls for independence threatening to dismantle France's sub-Saharan empire, French national pride demanded the retention of Algeria, whose rebellion was regarded a civil war. To concentrate on Algeria, the Socialist government of Prime Minister Guy Mollet acceded to

Moroccan demands for independence in spring 1956. Mollet could not have failed to realize that Tunisian demands for similar treatment would follow and would be all but impossible to reject. Bourguiba did, indeed, seize the opportunity to demand the termination of the Tunisian protectorate. France agreed and officially granted independence to Tunisia on March 20, 1956.

National elections for a Constituent Assembly held within a week returned a substantial Neo-Dustur majority, but a large number of abstentions, particularly in such Yusufist strongholds as Jarba, reminded the party of the need to proceed cautiously. Bourguiba entered the government as prime minister, his first official position in more than a quarter century of political activism. In August 1957, the Constituent Assembly deposed Amin Bey and declared the formation of a republic. It named Bourguiba president of the republic and vested in him many of the executive prerogatives formerly exercised by the bey.

NOTES

1. By the mid-1920s, almost half of all salaried workers in Tunisia were Europeans, according to Iqbal Ahmad and Stuart Schaar, "M'hamed Ali and the Tunisian Labour Movement," in *Race and Class* 19, no. 3 (Winter 1978):260.

2. According to Hafidh Sethom, "La Vie rurale de la Tunisie contemporaine: Etude historique et géographique," *Les Cahiers de Tunisie* 14 (1966):203, French estates averaged between 500 and 650 acres; Italian farms just over 100 acres; and Tunisian plots about 15 acres. As averages, the figures can be deceptive, but they reveal the magnitude of the French agricultural enterprise in Tunisia in the interwar period.

3. Some Tunisians with Neo-Dustur affiliations did collaborate with Germany during the war. Most of their actions, however, were expressions of vehement anti-French sentiments, rather than pro-Nazi ones.

9

Social Change Since 1956

The termination of the protectorate altered the first priority of the Neo-Dustur from political activism to social change. With independence won, Bourguiba and his associates set about instilling the values of modernity and progress—concepts their liberal French training had taught them to regard highly. Future generations of Tunisians were to be well educated and free of the limitations inherent in clinging to beliefs and practices made obsolete by contemporary world realities. The success of the modernizers hinged on the readiness of ordinary Tunisians to accept the need for and advantages of significant social change.

But most Tunisians derived their social perspective from a fundamentally different source than did the Western-educated elites. They put greater stock, for example, in traditional Islamic institutions and practices; in contrast, the secular Neo-Dustur leadership viewed these as impediments to society's advancement. Aware of the conservative nature of most Tunisians, Bourguiba assured them that he had no intention of attacking religion per se and frequently recalled his record of defending Islam against French efforts to weaken it during the nationalist era.[1] Rather, he maintained that a reassessment of Islamic institutions taking twentieth-century circumstances into account would invigorate the faith by strengthening its capacity to act as a vehicle for social progress. As further proof of official benevolence, independent Tunisia's constitution, promulgated in 1959, made Islam the state religion, although it guaranteed freedom of worship to practitioners of other faiths. Neo-Dustur–prompted changes in traditional Islamic practices laid the groundwork for societal transformation in related areas, most notably in the nature and role of education, the availability of medical care, and the status of women. These reforms created a more liberal, open, and progressive atmosphere than existed in countries in which traditionalism remained the norm.

117

The Tunisian drive for social change inspired similar trends in other Arab countries and served as a model for many Third World states.

ISLAM

The popular enthusiasm for Bourguiba and for the Neo-Dustur following independence accounts for the generally positive reception initially given reforms concerning Islam. Another factor facilitating change was the inability of the ulama, the guardians of tradition, to influence the course of events. The protectorate's co-option and intimidation of large numbers of ulama had discredited the religious leaders in the eyes of many Tunisians. Moreover, since the 1880s the nationalists, not the ulama, had customarily risen to the defense of Tunisia's Islamic legacy. Finally, the willingness of the rector of the Zaituna mosque-university—the most important Islamic institution in the country—to sanction Bourguiba's ideas gave them a religious seal of approval.

One of the earliest targets for reform was the Habus Administration, an agency particularly tainted by its collaboration with the French in supplying land for colonization. In 1956 the state seized public habus land, whose revenues normally supported mosques and other religious enterprises. In assuming responsibility for the finances of the many mosques and schools dependent on habus revenues, the government brought them under its control. Public habus land, along with abandoned colon estates, formed the basis for state-sponsored cooperative farms for landless peasants. In the following year, a second law ordered that private habus land (whose profits accrued to the individual creating the habus and to his descendants, although they no longer legally owned the land) be divided among the founder's heirs as private property.

The Neo-Dustur government also moved quickly to create a unified judiciary system by abolishing both the Islamic sharia courts and the French tribunals established during the protectorate. The closure of the religious courts paved the way for the introduction of a Personal Status Code outlawing many practices allowed by the sharia but regarded by modernists as discriminatory. The code reflected the Neo-Dustur conviction that traditional usages relegating women to an inferior social status and denying them basic rights thwarted national development. Further legislation in 1959 introduced civil and commercial codes derived from Western legal concepts. These laws continued the erosion of sharia law, as did the passage of a similar criminal code in 1968. Naturally, such fundamental changes affecting the entire population did not take root overnight. They gained more rapid acceptance in urban areas with longer and more intensive exposure to the West than in rural regions in which both men and women often clung tenaciously to tradition.

The Neo-Dustur also saw the need for a unified and centralized education system. It wanted the state to establish goals, prescribe methods of instruction, and monitor the operation of all schools, including religious ones. A 1956 decision to make religious educational institutions—from children's Quranic schools to the Zaituna mosque-university—part of the public education system epitomized this view. On one hand, to quiet fears that the Neo-Dustur intended to eliminate religious education, Bourguiba praised the Islamic schools for preserving Tunisian culture by resisting the efforts of protectorate officials to Gallicize them. On the other hand, he argued that the needs of the independent state required a thorough revamping of school curricula rather than the maintenance of traditional courses and techniques. In his estimation, the state could execute this task better than the ulama.

The first signs of opposition to the government's Islamic policies appeared in 1960 and 1961. In both years, Bourguiba encouraged Tunisians to ignore the Muslim obligation to fast during the daylight hours of the holy month of Ramadan. He argued that Tunisia could not afford the decline in productivity occasioned by this observance. To make his proposal more palatable, Bourguiba asserted that Tunisia was engaged in a jihad (a religiously sanctioned struggle) against underdevelopment and that Islam excused participants in a jihad from fasting. However, Bourguiba miscalculated the depth of popular attachment to tradition: Almost all Tunisians observed the fast. Even those who were not particularly religious regarded Ramadan and the various festivities and customs associated with it as symbols of their Arabo-Islamic heritage. Even in the upper echelons of the Neo-Dustur, Bourguiba's public breaking of the fast and his urging of others to do likewise had limited support. Many religious leaders openly rejected Bourguiba's reinterpretation of Ramadan, which they considered the last straw in a series of government infringements on religion. Most of those criticizing Bourguiba were quickly removed from their posts.

Just before Ramadan in 1961, antigovernment demonstrations erupted in Kairouan—a city whose links to North Africa's first Muslims gave it a special religious significance. After crushing these protests, Bourguiba tried to impugn the motives of their religious organizers with a suggestion that economic considerations—such as the ulama's loss of control over habus land—not religious matters, accounted for their antipathy toward the secular authorities. This charge contained an element of truth, but it misrepresented the primary concerns of most of the demonstrators. Despite his public statements, Bourguiba understood the signal sent by the Kairouan disorders: that he could go only so far in imposing his ideas about religion without creating a dangerous backlash.

Bourguiba continued to denigrate the Ramadan fast, but, not thinking the issue important enough to provoke a showdown with his critics, he abandoned the attempt to impose his view on an unwilling population. By 1961 the government had already dismantled or curbed much of the religious establishment and could deal with the remainder as long as it did not go too far. In fact, the state was anxious to decrease its direct involvement in Islamic affairs because its primary concerns were shifting to economic development. The virulence of the Neo-Dustur attack on Islamic institutions in the late 1950s eliminated for many years any possibility of a religiously based opposition to the regime. It also explains the appeal of Islamic opposition movements to devout Muslims of the 1970s and 1980s who believed that forsaking Islamic principles had caused and then aggravated the political and economic problems afflicting the country.

EDUCATION

Perhaps because high-quality educations had usually played a part in their own rise of prominence, Neo-Dustur leaders placed great stock in the importance of public education and worked to make it widely and freely available. They believed that an educated citizenry would better understand the desirability of the transformations they envisioned in Tunisian society. Moreover, a reasonably well-educated labor force was important for the success of the party's development programs. On a more abstract level, they expected widespread education to instill a sorely needed sense of national identity as the newly independent state took shape. All schools were nationalized in 1956, and a 1958 law made public education free to all Tunisians, although it did not mandate school attendance. Since independence, the government has consistently allocated between 25 percent and 30 percent of its budget for education, a high figure for a developing nation and a clear indication of its strong commitment to education as a central aspect of national development.

As Tunisians recognized the centrality of education in achieving upward mobility, school enrollments at all levels increased. The number of children in primary school (ages six to eleven), for example, rose fivefold in the first twenty years of independence. By the 1970s, three-quarters of all primary-school-aged children and 40 percent of those of secondary school age (twelve to seventeen years) were enrolled

Adult literacy class. (Photo courtesy of Lewis B. Ware)

in school. In 1956, by contrast, the figure for the latter group had been a mere 10 percent. However, only about 6 percent of secondary students completed the entire six-year course. Most took a certificate after three years and either entered the job market or pursued some form of specialized, nonacademic training.

Efforts to improve the quality of education by regulating advancement with competitive examinations brought about a decline in enrollments after the mid-1970s. At the same time, the government instituted new technical training programs, especially in agriculture and industry, to provide students with a fundamentally sound education while preparing them for jobs contributing to national economic development. This arrangement has created an elitist system, detrimental to children from poor and rural backgrounds with frequently substandard educations; the latter group cannot compete successfully with the better trained students of the urban middle class.

Tunisia's colonial legacy presented the country's leaders with a dilemma concerning the appropriate language of instruction in the schools. Bourguiba and his colleagues leaned toward an education system patterned on the French model and utilizing the French language. Their own training in a French milieu led them in this direction, but the use of French also accorded with their secular outlook. Arabic was closely associated with religious instruction, whereas French had been the language of modern, scientific education since before the protectorate. They knew that they could not entirely ignore the country's native tongue, but they were equally certain that favoring Arabic over French would hamper Tunisia's development, much of which hinged on access to and an understanding of Western technology and culture.

Consequently, a bilingual system evolved. Instruction in French was the norm at the university and in the secondary schools. For some years after independence, the Education Ministry relied on French nationals to staff teaching positions at those levels in the absence of enough qualified Tunisians. A mixture of the two languages, with Arabic theoretically gradually replacing French, prevailed at the primary level. Twenty years after independence, however, only the first two years of primary school had been fully Arabized, whereas at the secondary level some subjects (notably history, geography, and philosophy) were taught largely or exclusively in Arabic, but instruction in others remained in French.

Party leaders have periodically restated their support for the wider use of Arabic throughout society, but most of Tunisia's elites remain comfortable with French and have at best ambivalent feelings about replacing it with Arabic. As long as French remains the virtually exclusive medium for the transaction of important government and business matters, the elites' command of the language assures them a privileged position. If Arabic were to be used more extensively in these areas, the ranks of the elite would open to non-French speakers and jeopardize that privileged position.

Not surprisingly, then, the generation of future elites has always been far more receptive to Arabization, and support for it initially coalesced among secondary-school and university students. As early as the 1960s, they criticized the artificial ascendancy of French and half-hearted government efforts to promote bilingualism, claiming that such practices had left them with inadequate training in both languages. Students in the next decade further advanced the cause. Angered by social inequities they blamed on economic policies imported from the West and by Western support for a government growing less tolerant of dissent, these young men and women identified more closely than their predecessors with the Arabo-Islamic world, heightening their affinity for Arabic. They condemned Tunisia's French educational system as a manifestation of cultural imperialism and attributed the elites' lack of interest in Arabic to a general decline in traditional values stemming from the corrupt influence of the West. As Islamic opposition movements with similar views emerged in the

1970s, demands to rethink national language policies became more organized and more vocal, compelling even the strongest supporters of French to modulate their stands. Arabization was speeded up in the 1980s, with the greatest gains coming at the primary level.

The original postindependence concept of expanding Tunisians' educational opportunities has raised the national literacy rate to over 60 percent, one of the highest in the Arab world. But greater access to better education has also created higher expectations, which only steady economic growth and continuing societal development can fulfill. Since the 1970s, the number of young people leaving the schools has consistently exceeded the absorptive capacity of the economy, creating a potentially explosive situation. Youths unable to find work commensurate with their training experience bitter disappointment and frustration. The anger of other unfortunate men and women who, despite some education, can find no employment at all in the stagnant economy is even greater. Increasingly, such persons have turned to some form of political protest, flocking to the opposition movements that surfaced in the 1970s and forming the core of the antigovernment demonstrators in the bloody riots of 1978, 1980, and 1984. The disillusion of Tunisian youths who have benefited from some aspects of social change but have been unable to reap corresponding economic gains remains a key element of the country's instability.

MEDICAL CARE

Most Tunisians' access to medical attention reached a low ebb immediately after independence. The bulk of the country's physicians were Europeans, many of whom left in 1956 or shortly after. The few Tunisian doctors were clustered in the capital and, to a lesser extent, in regional cities like Sfax and Bizerte. To maximize the limited human resources available, the government required all physicians to devote specified portions of their time to service in public health facilities. This unpopular practice ended in 1969, partly because of a shift away from socialistic practices but also because students of the medical school established at the University of Tunis in 1964 were beginning to complete their training, thus augmenting the number of doctors. The medical school could not, however, provide enough doctors to staff the many clinics and dispensaries constructed in rural areas and small villages in the 1950s and 1960s as part of the government's campaign to improve living standards throughout the country. To close this gap, the government was compelled to contract for the services of doctors from abroad, a practice that has decreased in recent years but still continues.

By the 1980s, Tunisia's government-operated health care system consisted of some 100 hospitals and 500 local clinics. With approximately 1,800 doctors (one for every 3,700 persons), 330 dentists, 6,900 nurses, and 800 pharmacists, Tunisia's medical resources compared very favorably with those of its North African neighbors on a per capita basis but lagged behind those of most other countries in the Arab world. The attention paid to expanding and upgrading medical facilities, along with Ministry of Health campaigns for health education and the dissemination of information on preventive medicine, has contributed to halving the infant mortality rate since independence. Life expectancy at birth has risen over the same period from forty-six years to sixty years, a figure exceeded in the Arab world only in Jordan, Syria, and a few of the small states of the Gulf.

WOMEN IN INDEPENDENT TUNISIA

The Neo-Dustur leaders believed that assigning women to a secondary place in society failed to capitalize on one of Tunisia's most valuable commodities—its human resources. The priority accorded to the passage of the Personal Status Code of 1956 showed the importance the party attached to raising women's status and promoting their full participation in the nation's development. The Western-educated Neo-Dusturians were not, however, the first Tunisians to advocate such changes. In the 1930s, the Islamic reformer Tahar Haddad had presented a bold, liberal interpretation of Quranic passages regarding women. The conservative Zaituna ulama criticized Haddad and did all they could to prevent the dissemination of his views, but his ideas appealed to the young men of the Neo-Dustur. After coming to power, they evoked many of Haddad's themes to explain the changes they were introducing as modern renditions of Islamic customs.

Personal Status Code of 1956

The code was a daring undertaking. It attacked literal and traditional interpretations of Islam more vigorously than had occurred anywhere in the Muslim world except for the highly secularized Turkey of Mustafa Kemal Ataturk. Some of its articles had primarily symbolic value. The ban on polygyny, for example, affected only the 3 percent of the population still involved in multiple marriages, but it ended a deeply rooted tradition distinguishing Islamic societies from Western ones. Other aspects of the code had a much wider impact. Its requirement that women consent to marriage transformed that institution from a contractual arrangement between families to a voluntary union of individuals. The code also set minimum ages for marriage. These two provisions undermined the power of the extended, patriarchal family by making it more difficult for parents to follow the traditional practice of arranging marriages without taking the wishes of the prospective bride into account. This move fit nicely with a conscious state campaign to bolster the concept of the nuclear family, seen as a more appropriate grouping for modern societies than the extended family.

Some features of the code, such as those superseding Quranic regulations on inheritance, made women more independent and secure. Traditionally, females did not inherit equally with their male relatives, and although the new legislation did not establish complete equality between the sexes, it did increase women's shares. Another important change involved the tradition of a husband unilaterally repudiating his wife and dissolving their marriage by oral declaration. With the passage of the Personal Status Code, either party to a marriage had the right to institute divorce proceedings in the courts, which now had the sole power to terminate marriages. Finally, the new legislation abolished the restrictions on interfaith marriages that had prevented Muslim women from marrying non-Muslims.

With this sweeping official act, the Neo-Dustur government legislated away many inequities facing Tunisian women. Private attitudes concerning marriage, divorce, inheritance, and general male-female relationships could not be adjusted as easily or as rapidly as the law could be changed. Because the Personal Status Code so abruptly halted traditional practices and imposed such dramatically new behavioral standards on crucial areas of daily life, it gained neither universal nor immediate acceptance. Many ulama disapproved of the code, but the government onslaught of the late 1950s weakened them and they lacked adequate popular support to mount an effective resistance. Many Tunisian males, deprived of certain "rights" in their dealings with women, felt threatened by the new arrangements and avoided complying whenever they could. Not even all women welcomed the code's passage; many hesitated to abandon long-established practices with which they were comfortable. Even though the code theoretically improved their lot, adhering to it required a mental leap that many women, especially those with traditional backgrounds, simply could not make. As a result, the code was hard to enforce and often presented the authorities with delicate situations.

The Personal Status Code placed the Neo-Dustur government's advocacy of social change on the record quickly and unambiguously.

Party officials realized, however, that they would encounter difficulties if they attempted to restructure the society exclusively by legislative fiat. They believed that better, more modern educations for both males and females were the best means of producing a national atmosphere conducive to social change and modernization. Schooling was mandatory only for boys, but parents were encouraged to enroll their daughters as well. Although the percentage of females in the school population has never equaled the more than 50 percent of the total population that women constitute, by the 1980s some 40 percent of all primary school students were girls. At the secondary and university levels the figures dropped to 28 percent and 23 percent, respectively. To informally educate women and lobby for their basic rights, the party sponsored the creation of the Union Nationale des Femmes Tunisiennes (UNFT) in 1956.

Social Changes

To avoid a backlash from imposing too many changes too quickly, the government sought to foster other new ideas by persuasion and education rather than by law. Its campaign against traditional forms of dress, particularly the veil, exemplified this approach. Modernists like Bourguiba thought that wearing traditional clothing fostered traditional thinking; that the veil was demeaning to women who wore it; and that many traditional garments (for both men and women) were cumbersome or simply inappropriate in modern societies. Public criticism of veiling began as early as 1957. Bourguiba rightly argued that Islam did not require the veiling of women, stressing that there was nothing immoral or un-Islamic in Tunisian women shedding their traditional face coverings. He did not, however, ban any form of clothing completely, as Ataturk had done in Turkey in the 1920s. A law that forbade female students to wear the veil in the classroom did not apply beyond the school. Nevertheless, the government made clear its preference that young women not veil themselves.

Although Western dress and habits spread among Tunisian women after independence, traditional clothing has never entirely disappeared from the streets, much less from the home. As in most matters of social transformation, the effort to end veiling met with greater success in urban than in rural areas (even though the practice had always been more common among city women) and among younger women than older ones, who found it difficult to give up lifelong traditions and habits associated with morality and proper behavior.

In addition to these consciously designed programs, other social and economic circumstances brought change to the lives of Tunisian

Women wearing traditional *saf-saris*. (Photo courtesy of Lewis B. Ware)

women. The severe housing shortages accompanying the rapid urbanization of independent Tunisia contributed to the decline of the extended family. In the nuclear family, women often took over responsibilities traditionally reserved for men. Economic hardship compelled many women who would not otherwise have worked outside the home to enter the labor force, an experience inevitably changing their view of the world. Finally, the extensive development of tourism and easy access to mass media familiarized Tunisian women (and men) with the world beyond their immediate horizons more fully than ever before. Television, radio, and the press gave glimpses of women in other parts of the world, who often served as role models for Tunisian women.

In the 1970s, the momentum for social change slowed. The party's old guard (males in their fifties and sixties) who ruled the country registered alarm at the assertiveness of certain segments of the society, including women and the young, which were seeking to parlay their advances in the 1960s into increased political power. Thus threatened, the veteran politicians moved to protect the status quo, creating a highly polarized situation. Bourguiba's chastisement of party members agitating for more liberal policies at the 1974 party congress confirmed this approach.

Planned, government-sponsored programs fostering social change dwindled. Women's education, for example, received less emphasis in the 1970s than at any time since independence. This pleased conservative critics who objected to women's education in principle. Rising unemployment also fueled prejudices against women. Men, especially those with minimal educations, feared them as competitors for jobs they, as heads of families, needed for psychological as well as economic reasons. Despite this retrenchment—and it must be noted that even in the 1970s the percentage of Tunisian women in school exceeded figures for most Arab states—other processes producing great social changes as byproducts, such as urbanization, industrialization, and tourism, continued at a rapid pace, to some extent offsetting the government's inaction.

Attacks on women's education were manifestations of the popular disenchantment, growing stronger in the mid-1970s, with the imported philosophies that many Tunisians believed were destroying the nation. A countervailing effort to reinvigorate indigenous traditions greatly contributed to the emergence of Islamic organizations demanding greater respect for Arabo-Islamic values. From the outset, these groups attracted many women, especially university or secondary-school students. Some women may have affiliated with the Islamic groups primarily because they represented one of the few available means of opposing the regime, rather than out of sympathy with their ideology. Many others, however, sincerely believed that government policies had undermined the moral and religious values traditional practices kept alive. That these changes had been forced on them in the name of progress—as defined from outside their own culture—but that they had experienced few tangible benefits from them added to their anger.

Many women adherents of the Islamic organizations adopted the practice of wearing traditional clothing, including the veil, to symbolize their rejection of foreign influences and their commitment to traditional values rooted in popular interpretations of Islam. Earlier government efforts to limit the use of the veil have made its reappearance since the mid-1970s an act of defiance as well as of protest. The adoption of the veil by young educated women who had not worn it before revealed the extent to which distress over the spread of alien cultural values had permeated Tunisian society.

Family Planning

Another source of controversy involving women has been family planning, also an imported practice. The government voiced strong support for birth control after 1956: Bourguiba publicly reasoned that Tunisia's transformation into a modern industrial nation would occur more smoothly and have a more immediately beneficial impact if the population did not expand too rapidly. He also knew that, without some restraints on growth, the nation's population would quickly outstrip its limited economic resources. The first halting steps toward coping with demographic issues came in the Personal Status Code. It prohibited families from claiming government allowances for more than four children and legalized abortions for mothers of five or more children. A 1973 law made all women eligible for abortions, but the government clearly stated that it did not regard abortion as a viable long-term solution to overpopulation.

A systematic family-planning program was begun in 1964; it included the distribution of birth control devices and an educational campaign to familiarize women with their use and to inform them of the advantages of limiting family size. The first of its kind in Africa, this initiative was, like the Personal Status Code, a daring and ambitious move. Although Islam does not forbid birth control, traditional beliefs had made the practice uncommon in Tunisia, as in most non-Western societies. Even as strong a defender of women's rights as Tahar Haddad had stressed the duty of women to bear children, a view in accord with the thinking of most Tunisians in the mid-twentieth century.

Traditionally, Tunisians regarded large families as a sign of God's blessing: They established the husband's virility and guaranteed that the parents would be cared for in the twilight of their lives. Before the advent of mechanized agriculture, and even thereafter for the many untouched by it, large families facilitated the working of the land. Ironically, however, Quranic inheritance laws resulted in the subdivision of land into plots so small that they were virtually useless if the heirs were too numerous. Recurrent natural disasters combined with poor health and sanitary conditions to produce an extremely high infant mortality rate. To counter this situation, families customarily produced a large number of children to ensure the survival of as many as possible. As European influences increased, and particularly with the onset of Western political domination, some colonized people viewed the promotion of birth control as an imperial plot to keep their populations small and manageable.

Traditional attitudes such as these hampered the family-planning program, but its overly ambitious scope proved an equally serious drawback. In attempting to make their services immediately available to all Tunisian women, the project's organizers spread their resources too thin. The limited and not always adequately trained staff could rarely provide the important follow-up necessary to ensure that women given birth control devices utilized them properly. Despite these problems, the program showed real promise for curbing population growth. In fact, not long after its inception, some government officials began to have second thoughts about the wisdom of family planning. They feared that the stabilization of Tunisia's population, which was already much smaller than that of any of its North African neighbors except Libya, would limit the country's impact on Maghribi affairs. Although never explicitly acknowledged, fear of a popular reaction against government meddling in so private an area may also have raised doubts about the advisability of continuing a full-scale birth control campaign. As a result, the family-planning program was pared down even before the retrenchment in other social services in the 1970s.

It was not entirely abandoned, however, and the decision to limit it actually heightened its efficacy. When Tunisia turned from socialist to capitalist forms of development in the 1970s, Western economic assistance increased. Since then, the U.S. Agency for International Development (USAID) and similar organizations have provided substantial funds for family planning. The crude birth rate has declined to one of the lowest in the Arab world, and demographers estimate that by the end of the century it will compare favorably with those of European Mediterranean countries. As in other areas of social change, class and economic status have influenced women's receptivity to family planning. Middle- and upper-class women, those with modern educations, and those residing in urban areas have responded more positively and more rapidly to the concept than have rural peasant women.

The economic, social, and political status of Tunisian women has improved greatly since 1956, although in no area have women achieved complete parity with men. Since the mid-1970s, however, the government has shown less interest in the kinds of dramatic measures affecting women that characterized the earlier years of independence. It has taken this stand, in large part, to avoid provoking its traditionalist opponents. Although some women have applauded this reversal, many westernized women have fallen out with the party, accusing it of reneging on its commitments. They have also criticized Tunisia's Western supporters for accepting the progressive image of the country the government puts forward, claiming that it rests on past accomplishments rather than current policies.

NOTES

1. Bourguiba's attitude toward Islam has always been essentially opportunistic: He supported or opposed it according to prevailing political situations. His actions suggest the label *nonreligious*, but not *antireligious*.

10

The Tunisian Economy Since 1956

Economic development, including industrialization, was a major objective of the postindependence government as it sought to establish Tunisia's place in the modern world. Protectorate officials had done so little to encourage industry that in 1956 less than 2 percent of the Tunisian population held jobs in manufacturing. The economy rested, as it traditionally had, on agriculture, and Europeans dominated all sectors well out of proportion to their small numbers. They monopolized managerial positions; owned almost a fifth of the country's cultivable land, most of it in the rich Majarda Valley; and produced about 40 percent of Tunisia's crops. Although some colons left the country during the violence preceding independence and others when the protectorate ended, no general exodus of settlers took place.

Despite this economic situation, the need for social change received the Neo-Dustur's highest priority after independence. To avoid diverting attention from social reforms, the party chose not to tamper with the liberal economy but to maintain close ties with France and to allow the former colons to retain their holdings. The UGTT, led by Ahmad Ben Salah since Hashid's assassination, disagreed and called for a policy of economic planning and socialism. The union had stood by Bourguiba in the Ben Yusuf affair, and four of its top officials held ministerial positions in the first independent government, making it difficult for the Neo-Dustur to ignore its views. Nevertheless, party chieftains feared that such an approach would scare away potential investors. Ben Salah refused to endorse the party's decision and resigned as UGTT secretary general. The Neo-Dustur quickly moved to bring the union more firmly under its control. To the chagrin of the advocates of a free economy, however, investment declined sharply and substantial profits were transferred out of the country in the late 1950s, as investors remained uncertain that the laissez-faire philosophy would prevail. To compensate, the government relied heavily on foreign aid, especially from France and the United States.

Early experiments in land reform illustrate the Neo-Dustur's efforts to achieve social reconstruction while retaining liberal economic principles. Between 1956 and 1963, the government seized abandoned colon lands and offered to purchase estates still in European hands in order to create cooperative farms providing landless peasants access to mechanized equipment and easy credit. Very often, the small holdings of Tunisian farmers adjacent to the former colon estates were merged into the co-ops. In this case, owners retained the title to their lands, and resettled peasants received titles for the first time. Private ownership was the rule, but management decisions intended to increase yields and diversify production were taken collectively.

ECONOMIC PLANNING AND SOCIALISM
IN THE 1960s

As the stagnant economy showed no sign of improving, party members, especially those affiliated with the UGTT, demanded that a stimulus for economic growth be found. In 1961, reversing his earlier stand, Bourguiba appointed Ben Salah to head a newly formed Ministry of Planning to upgrade the state's role in the economy and devise socialist development strategies. In the following year Ben Salah unveiled a Ten-Year Plan to foster self-sufficiency and raise living standards. The blueprint encountered opposition from farmers and small businesspeople who worried that state intervention would restrict their freedom to operate their enterprises as they saw fit, but Bourguiba's vigorous support for the plan temporarily silenced most critics. The renaming of the Neo-Dustur as the Parti Socialiste Dusturien (Dusturian Socialist Party, or PSD) in 1964 symbolized its commitment to the new policies.

Ben Salah's planning team believed that the complete decolonization of the economy was an essential step toward its goals. The ministry oversaw the construction of new state-owned factories across the country, particularly in provincial urban centers. This was an effort not only to decrease Tunisian reliance on foreign goods but also to balance the colonial practice of confining most of the limited industrialization that had occurred to the Tunis region. Officials hoped to achieve a more uniform pattern of development benefiting previously overlooked parts of the country. After independence, large numbers of provincial urbanites had moved to Tunis, lured by the attractive

Olive grove in the Sahil. (Photo courtesy of Lewis B. Ware)

jobs—of types unavailable in their home towns—coming vacant as foreigners left the capital. The percentage of foreigners living in Tunis dropped from a third of the city's population in 1956 to a mere 4 percent a decade later.

This drain of talented human resources had heightened the already considerable disadvantages of the secondary and tertiary communities. Planners hoped that their infusion of new economic opportunities into the hinterland would halt this damaging trend.

The industrial sector did expand under Ben Salah's tutelage. Phosphate production, in a slump since before World War II, revived as the government built treatment and processing plants capable of exporting phosphate products that were more lucrative than the raw mineral. In 1966, the start of production in Saharan oil fields prompted the construction of a refinery, which lessened Tunisia's need to import the petroleum products crucial to industrialization. Similarly, steel mills and cement factories boosted national self-sufficiency by supplying essential materials for the building boom then under way.

Because the agricultural sector at the heart of the Tunisian economy did not provide enough jobs for the steadily and rapidly growing population, many rural Tunisians left the countryside in search of employment in factories in the cities. The high-profile, capital-intensive projects of the 1960s gave rise to the image of a burgeoning, industrializing economy, but they created relatively few new jobs. Consequently, urban unemployment posed a growing problem. Those who did hold industrial jobs found serious flaws in the government's policies. Only once in the decade, for example, did the guaranteed minimum salary increase, despite price hikes averaging 3.5 percent annually. The Neo-Dustur's strong control over the UGTT prevented the union from speaking out on behalf of the workers, severely discrediting it in their eyes.

The most dramatic example of economic decolonization was the 1964 confiscation of land still in European hands. These estates formed the bases for new agricultural cooperatives. At the same time, the Planning Ministry ordered many peasants with small holdings to organize cooperatives. The planners' hope was that these state farms would meet the nation's food requirements more efficiently, provide reasonably predictable quantities of exportable foodstuffs, and keep the rural population on the land and arrest the growth of the cities. By the late 1960s, cooperatives accounted for more than one-third of Tunisia's cultivable land and employed almost one-third of the rural population.

The Planning Ministry, however, had great difficulty implementing its policies in the agricultural sector. Ben Salah's passion for the cooperatives led to charges that he favored eliminating all private capital, an accusation adding to the ranks of his opponents, especially among middle- and large-scale farmers who wanted nothing to do with state control. The peasants drawn into the cooperatives also disliked them. Above all, they resented the loss of their plots, no matter how small or marginal. The centralized decisionmaking necessarily involved in the cooperatives irritated them, especially since many of the farms' administrators were ministry technocrats with limited knowledge of rural life, land management, or marketing techniques. The peasants often complained of overcrowded conditions resulting from the consolidation of too large a number of holdings, each of which traditionally supported a large family.

Many peasants concluded that, rather than improving their lot, the cooperatives left them worse off. To maximize state profits, the government paid artificially low prices for goods from the cooperatives, resulting in a decline in their producers' real income. With reason, the peasants regarded the city dwellers enjoying lower food prices as the primary beneficiaries of the system. The economic gap between rural and urban areas widened as the government continued to provide advantages to the restless, potentially more troublesome urbanites at the expense of rural interests. To worsen the peasants' plight, the loss of their land and their animals left them with no other option than to sell their own labor in circumstances they could not control.

Other problems, including high operating expenses, plagued the cooperatives. The poor condition of much of the land brought into the system made substantial investments necessary to make it productive, but the cooperatives met with so little enthusiasm that few of the state's investments were ever returned. Much of the initial cost of setting up the cooperatives was defrayed by contracting foreign loans whose repayment burdened the treasury. By increasing the country's international debt, these loans tied it closely to the world economy, contradicting the Planning Ministry's goal of diminishing economic dependence. No international agency provided extensive support for the cooperative venture. On the contrary, French aid decreased after 1964, reflecting anger over the confiscation of French citizens' land. Extremely poor weather resulted in a succession of disastrous harvests from 1964 to 1968. Cooperative productivity fell drastically, and by the latter year four out of five cooperatives regularly lost money. The financial onus imposed on Tunisia by collectivization contributed significantly to the experiment's ultimate collapse.

Ben Salah insisted on pursuing his policies despite mounting opposition and their obvious shortcomings. His decision to collectivize the rich olive groves owned mostly by middle-class Sahil farmers sent shock waves throughout the private agricultural sector. The Planning Ministry's 1969 announcement that it was taking steps to bring all cultivable land under state control raised a popular outcry that Tunisia's leaders could not ignore. The government backed away from the proposal and, more important, allowed farmers to withdraw from the cooperatives. Virtually all did. The decimated cooperative system was reduced almost overnight to the state-owned land of former colon farms.

Bourguiba, anxious that blame for the problems associated with the cooperatives fall outside the presidential palace, charged Ben Salah with deliberately misleading him and subordinating the well-being of the rural population to his zeal to collectivize agriculture. Rumors that Ben Salah had condoned corrupt practices within the Planning Ministry further undermined his position. But perhaps Ben Salah's most serious offense in the eyes of the political leadership was his alienation of many long-time supporters of the Neo-Dustur, especially workers, peasants, and small businesspeople. Tried on charges of treason, the former minister was convicted and imprisoned. He escaped in 1973 and fled abroad, where he formed an exile opposition movement.

ECONOMIC LIBERALISM IN THE 1970s

Ben Salah's downfall allowed his PSD critics to reassert their influence, precipitating a major reorganization of the economy. With the government perilously close to bankruptcy, only generous foreign aid and infusions of private capital were thought to be able to shore up the deteriorating situation. Although the state continued to operate enterprises set up in the 1960s and to invest in new projects, particularly heavy industries turning out primary products, it also worked to make private foreign investments as attractive as possible. The principal architect of this policy was Hadi Nuwaira, a trusted associate of Bourguiba and former director of the Tunisian Central Bank who became prime minister in 1970. After the previous decade's disasters, private investors required assurances of quick and substantial profits for any ventures they might finance. Nuwaira oversaw the enactment of legislation in 1972 authorizing tax exemptions and rebates, as well as duty-free import privileges, for investors establishing companies producing for export.

In formulating the first Five-Year Plan of the 1970s (1973–1977), the government stressed labor-intensive industries and anticipated that the creation of new jobs would be the primary contribution of most new investments made during the plan. Employment opportunities were clearly the greatest benefit of the "offshore" industries promoted by Nuwaira, since their products never reached Tunisian markets and their owners enjoyed considerable tax relief. On the whole, however, the decision to rely on private investors to create new jobs met with only relative success. The availability of places in the work force failed to keep pace with population growth, which hovered around 2 percent annually nationwide and was higher in the cities. Moreover, women who had not previously worked held many of the new jobs. Foreign employers did not share the reluctance of their Tunisian counterparts to hire women, whom they usually paid lower wages than men. These factors reduced the new industries' impact on unemployment, and many men remained out of work or underemployed.

Nevertheless, the liberal economy produced a dramatic growth spurt, with industry leading the way. Nuwaira's inducements led to the construction of over 500 foreign-owned factories between 1973 and 1978. At the end of the decade, the industrial sector accounted for 20 percent of all jobs, more than double the number it provided in the Ben Salah era. In the course of the 1970s, gross national product rose steadily, and national revenue doubled.

Carefully orchestrated government policies spurred the recovery, but crucial factors less susceptible to the authorities' control also figured prominently. Oil exports remained steady at about 4 million tons a year, but their value skyrocketed after the world energy crisis of 1973–1974. Income from petroleum exports increased more than tenfold during the 1970s, making oil Tunisia's primary source of revenue. Early in the following decade, when production had risen by another million tons annually, oil supplied some 16 percent of the state's funds. The possibility of exporting labor offered some relief for unemployment, and the remittances of Tunisians working abroad made a valuable contribution to the national income. Before the 1973 recession (also occasioned by the rise in oil prices), most excess labor migrated to France. Even toward the end of the decade, over 200,000 Tunisians (including workers' families) resided in France, although Libya had replaced the excolonial power as the primary outlet for the unemployed. Men from the south, where development projects had had less effect than in other areas and where poverty and unemployment were particularly acute, flocked to Libya. Finally, a succession of good harvests at the start of the 1970s helped agriculture to recover from the damage done by the cooperative experiment. The restoration of private property resulted in an almost immediate increase in rural productivity and profits, particularly for growers of export commodities.

There was, however, a price to be paid for the economic policies of the Nuwaira government. The decision to gear the economy toward exports rather than internal consumption, the heavy emphasis on foreign investments, and the willingness to lean on labor migration to temper unemployment—in short, the extroversion of the economy— had inherent dangers. Excessive dependence on foreign markets rendered Tunisia vulnerable to circumstances it could not influence. An oil glut on world markets, for example, lessened Tunisia's income, sending shock waves through an economy that had come to rely on substantial oil revenues for continued growth.

Citrus fruits and olives, the country's most important agricultural exports, faced high tariffs and other import restrictions imposed by the European Economic Community (EEC) to protect member state producers of the same goods. (Many Tunisian manufactured goods faced a similar fate as EEC members safeguarded domestic industries against cheaply produced foreign imports.) As closer ties developed between the EEC and Greece and Spain, whose agricultural exports virtually duplicated those of Tunisia, the problems of Tunisian farmers worsened. During the 1970s, the value of their exports rarely reached 50 percent of the value of agricultural imports. The need to fill recurrent domestic food shortages, occasioned by the stress on growing crops for export, kept the level of farm imports high.

Investors' desires for sizable and rapid profits caused an imbalanced development of the industrial sector. Many more businesses employing workers with minimal skills (such as textile mills and clothing factories) were built than were the more sophisticated plants (such as engineering concerns, food-processing factories, or medium-tech industries) that, though initially more expensive to staff and operate, would have better served Tunisian economic interests in the long run. The siting of new factories brought about another form of imbalance. Investors preferred to locate along the coast, especially around Tunis, where the supply of well-trained workers was greater than elsewhere. These same coastal zones also provided the easiest and cheapest access to the European markets. As a result, 90 percent of all new jobs in the 1970s were in these areas, compounding the unemployment problem in neglected regions (particularly the south, where very little industrialization occurred) and promoting the migration of rural Tunisians to the cities or abroad. Government efforts to disperse some of the new industries came only at the end of the decade, too late to reverse the damage already done.

Overseas labor migration relieved economic pressures only in the short term. It failed as a satisfactory permanent solution because it hinged on such critical variables as a prosperous economy in the host country and consistently good relations between host and supplier countries—neither of which Tunisia alone could ensure. Recessions in Europe cut back on the number of jobs available for guest workers. Disagreements between Tunisia and the host states could lead to the expulsion of laborers, with serious repercussions for an economy unable to absorb them. More subtly, host countries could threaten reprisals against guest workers to force Tunisia to adopt political or economic stands that they espoused but that did not conform with Tunisian interests. In the case of Tunisians working in Libya, the regime of Muammar Qaddafi took advantage of their anger with their government to promote revolutionary sentiments, going so far as to provide some with guerrilla training, making them a threat to order and stability when they returned to their homes, usually in the underdeveloped south.

In final analysis, the shift from the self-centered development of Ben Salah's authoritarian socialism to the extroversion of Nuwaira's economic liberalism created social traumas canceling many of the advantages of the economic growth achieved in the 1970s. A small number of Tunisian capitalists in a position to invest in new development schemes themselves, to form partnerships with foreign investors, or to provide services needed by the foreigners rapidly accumulated fortunes. Many of them were close to Prime Minister Nuwaira, who had cultivated excellent contacts with important private-sector businesspeople during his tenure as Central Bank director.

Most ordinary Tunisians did not fare as well. Average income rose almost 4 percent annually, but consumer prices climbed at twice that rate, driven up by increases in the production costs of local goods and by the influx of higher priced consumer-oriented imports that had accompanied liberalization. Expensive capital equipment needed for industrialization added substantially to Tunisia's import bill. Exports, on the other hand, rarely paid for more than 60 percent of imports, even after the price of oil, which constituted half of all exports by value, rose dramatically in 1973. The Nuwaira government attempted to offset the trade deficit by making Tunisian exports as cheap and competitive as possible, necessitating low salaries for Tunisian workers. Thus, despite a doubling of national revenue between 1970 and 1980, the percentage of revenue allocated to salaries actually declined. To compensate for low real wages, the government subsidized basic commodities, including cereals, cooking oil, sugar, and charcoal. As much as 15 percent of the state's expenditures went into such direct subventions, whereas state funds reducing the cost of housing, electricity, water, and health care constituted another 17 percent. Since oil-derived revenues largely financed the subsidies, the leveling of international oil prices toward the end of the decade placed them in jeopardy.

The economic situation of the 1970s made class disparities glaringly and painfully evident. Twenty percent of the inhabitants accounted for more than half of all funds spent by Tunisians, whereas the poorest 20 percent of the population accounted for a mere 5 percent of those total expenditures. The widening gap between haves and have-nots spawned jealousies and heightened tensions. Statistics on population and unemployment, which stood at about 13 percent nationwide, revealed different but equally dangerous disparities. Thirty-five percent of the people classified as potentially economically active were between fifteen and twenty-five years old. Yet men in this age group experienced an unemployment rate almost twice the national average and made up 60 percent of the ranks of the unemployed—an unsettling figure in a country in which approximately 60 percent of the population was under the age of twenty-five.

In the agricultural sector conditions also deteriorated. Many small farmers restored to their land after the dismantling of the cooperatives lacked sufficient capital (in both money and animals) to reestablish themselves successfully in the transformed economy. Those unable to produce substantial quantities of exportable goods accumulated debts that eventually forced them to sell their land. Wealthy, usually absentee investors acquired vast acreages on which they made maximum use of machinery and minimum use of human labor. Unable to make a living even as wage laborers on their former lands, many rural families fled to the cities, only to swell the ranks of the urban unemployed.[1]

The Nuwaira government tried to defuse criticisms of the dismal economic situation by stifling virtually all forms of protest. The UGTT, after lying dormant for much of the 1960s, was revived in response to the devastating problems its members faced in the wake of economic liberalization. Wildcat strikes in the early 1970s indicated that the party was losing its influence in the union, which had never been truly subservient to the Neo-Dustur but rather had striven to keep Tunisian political leaders attuned to the needs of the working class. Workers frequently ignored a 1973 government prohibition of strikes, and the authorities' use of the police and army to end the stoppages fueled their conviction that the PSD cared little about their problems. Aside from a brief and unsuccessful experiment in drawing up a social pact with workers in 1977, the government made no effort to redress labor's grievances.

UGTT Secretary General Habib Ashur found himself in a difficult position. His long association with organized labor left him sympathetic to the workers' demands, but Ashur also sat on the PSD Political Bureau. Officials of the party and the government pressured him to end the disruptions. Amid indications that the government was losing patience and was about to take harsh steps to curb it, the UGTT called a general strike—the first since independence—for January 26, 1978. The Black Thursday demonstrations degenerated into widespread violence with bitter clashes between workers and the police and army. Estimates of the fatalities sustained as government forces dispersed the strikers ranged between 50 and 200. Hundreds more, including Ashur, were arrested. This manifestation of deep worker antagonism placed the government on notice that many Tunisians were approaching the limits of toleration for existing policies. Two years later in Gafsa an armed insurrection (of Libyan inspiration) underscored the dangers of perpetuating the underdevelopment of an entire region. Frustrations of a political nature were an important component in precipitating both the Black Thursday and the Gafsa incidents, but Nuwaira's economic policies had created hardships that made the protests inevitable. The prime minister's death shortly after the raid on Gafsa provided an opportunity for the PSD to distance itself from the most extreme of Nuwaira's failed formulas.

THE SEARCH FOR AN ECONOMIC MIDDLE GROUND
IN THE 1980s

With the support of the aging Bourguiba, the new prime minister, Muhammad Mzali, sought compromises between the socialism of the 1960s and the liberalism of the 1970s to resolve Tunisia's most serious economic problems: unemployment, officially estimated at 13 percent but probably higher; inflation, running at about 13 percent annually; and egregious income differentials originating in the 1970s.

The Sixth Five-Year Plan (1982–1986) devoted more attention to agriculture than had its forerunners. Specifically, it called for increases in agricultural production, which would lessen the need for costly food imports. But the plan placed its strongest emphasis on developing a carefully thought out program of industrialization, still seen by the government as the only way to deal with the country's most fundamental economic problems. Foreign investments were encouraged, since not many Tunisians had sufficient capital to import the raw materials and machinery necessary to sustain industrialization. There was also an attempt to stimulate the economy by attracting new foreign investments in the service sector. The Middle East regional headquarters of some banks and multinational firms did relocate in Tunis when the chaos following the Israeli invasion of Lebanon in 1982 forced them to abandon their Beirut headquarters. Similarly, Egypt's ostracism from the Arab world after its peace treaty with Israel brought some Cairo-based enterprises to Tunis. The willingness of all of these businesses to remain, however, hinged on the country's long-term stability, thus adding to the pressures on the Mzali government to maintain order.

A severe drought and a particularly inadequate harvest in 1982 complicated early efforts to reinvigorate the economy. More damaging because of their residual impact were declines in earnings from both oil and phosphate sales. Such drops in revenue intensified the burden of government subsidies, which proved to be the most difficult problem facing Mzali. Although fearful of the popular hostility austerity measures were likely to generate, especially while wages remained low to guarantee the competitiveness of Tunisian products and the profits of foreign investors, the government succumbed to demands from the International Monetary Fund and other aid donors[2] to tighten its belt. It began to withdraw some subsidies and reduce others beginning in 1983.

The removal of government subsidies from bread and semolina in January 1984 raised the cost of these staples by 115 percent. Rioting, at first in the south but rapidly spreading everywhere, paralyzed the country for almost two weeks. A state of emergency was declared and again, as in 1978 and 1980, the restoration of order by the security forces cost many lives. Official reports, which placed the death toll at 89 with almost 1,000 injured, almost certainly underestimated casualties. The volatile mass of frustrated, unemployed workers formed the core of the demonstrators. Convinced that austerity measures hurt them far more than they did the better off segments of society, they demanded a more equitable solution to the nation's economic woes. Sympathizers of many of the political factions critical of the Bourguiba regime joined the rioters' ranks, hoping in vain that the disorders might topple the government. Despite the authorities' claims of conspiracy, the riots were neither preconceived nor centrally directed; instead, they were the spontaneous result of the government increasing economic and political pressures beyond the breaking point of the working class. The fundamental issue of fairness posed by the 1984 riots remains the central one facing the Mzali government in its search for methods of creating prosperity that do not achieve their objectives at the expense of the poorest and least influential segment of the society.

TOURISM AND THE TUNISIAN ECONOMY

Tunisia's "exotic" atmosphere, attractive climate, pleasant beaches, proximity to Europe and, until recently, political tranquillity have all helped make tourism an important facet of the economy. The 1.5 million foreign visitors to the country every year have generated 30,000 jobs in the hotel business and another 100,000 in services directly linked to tourism. Serious efforts to develop this industry date to the organization of the state run Société des Hôtels Tunisiens Touristiques (SHTT) in the 1960s. The first hotels and resort complexes designed to lure European visitors appeared along the east coast, with heavy concentrations on the island of Jarba and the areas of Sousse and Hammamet. Tourist hotels opened in towns along the northern coast and in the interior, particularly the Saharan oases, somewhat later. Within a decade, tourism accounted for 20 percent of Tunisia's foreign currency earnings, exceeded only by the sale of oil, which assumed first place after the price rises of 1973.

But tourism has proved a mixed blessing for Tunisia. As with other aspects of the extroversion of the economy, the success or failure of the industry depends upon circumstances beyond Tunisian control. Downturns in the economies of the European nations from which the bulk of the tourists come (although some are North Americans) reduce the number of individuals able to afford overseas vacations.

Political events, even those only peripherally concerning either the host country or the visitors' countries, can also affect tourism, as demonstrated in Tunisia by the Arab-Israeli War of June 1967. For the remainder of that summer, many Europeans were apprehensive about traveling in the Mediterranean area and about their security in Arab countries, in which anti-Western sentiments ran high in the wake of the war. Although this was not the case in Tunisia, President Bourguiba nevertheless felt obliged to try to avert the damages likely to result from a significant decline in tourist revenues by offering public assurances of the safety of foreign visitors to keep potential vacationers from canceling their plans. Westerners' anxiety about security in the wake of terrorist incidents in the Mediterranean and southern Europe in the mid-1980s had a similarly negative impact on tourism in Tunisia.

Extensive hotel construction on Jarba and around Hammamet and Sousse has widened the development gap between the coastal zone and the interior. It has also taken a severe toll on agriculture. Often built on land once farmed, the hotels and their auxiliary services have taken acreage out of production even though harvests have consistently fallen short of domestic needs. Moreover, the hotels compete with local farmers for water, which is used by their guests in prodigious daily quantities: Each tourist bed accounts for the consumption of some 100 gallons of water daily. Because hotels have driven up the cost of water beyond the means of many small farmers, more thousands of irrigated acres have been lost to production. Finally, the steady and relatively good wages paid by the hotels induced some local farmers to take jobs in them from the outset. Owing to the migration from rural areas, they could often find only bedouin laborers, barely familiar with irrigation or other farming techniques, to work their land for them. Almost invariably, production declined, and some of the small farms were ruined.

The better paying jobs in the tourist industry require certain skills, such as command of a European language, which most locally available workers lack. As a result, only the most menial jobs (maids, kitchen help, groundskeepers) are open to them, whereas young men and women from other parts of the country or even from abroad fill the more prestigious managerial positions. This labor division lessens the positive impact of the hotels on the local economy, but it also means that most Tunisians involved in tourism hold subservient positions requiring them to wait on foreign visitors. Many Tunisians view this arrangement with distaste, seeing it as an extension of colonialism, which also subordinated the needs and dignity of Tunisians to the whims of foreigners. The fact that few tourists have any interest

Beach resort near Sousse. (Photo by author)

in the Tunisians themselves but are concerned only with their own pleasure and the attractions of the physical setting reduces the workers to the status of embellishments on the landscape and further diminishes their self-esteem.

Critics of tourism have also made the point that certain of its aspects have challenged and undermined traditional Tunisian values. They charge that tourism—rendering hospitality upon payment of a fee—is the complete antithesis of the age-old Arab concept of obligatory hospitality for guests. The presence of large numbers of foreign visitors has exposed Tunisians to lifestyles, customs, and moral values at variance with their own. The relative wealth of the tourists arouses the jealousy of the workers who serve them and raises aspirations for material goods that their own society cannot yet satisfy. Western tourists' notions about proper public behavior between the sexes or what constitutes acceptable and modest attire (an issue particularly at beach resort settings or when scantily clad tourists visit mosques) are only two jarring examples of visitors' practices offensive to many Tunisians. Those who cherish traditional standards accuse the foreigners of insensitivity to Arabo-Islamic values and worry about the disruptive impact of alien norms, especially on young Tunisians. Spokespeople for the Islamic movement have vigorously criticized the corrosive effect of Western views on Tunisian society, blaming not only tourism but also the European films and radio and television broadcasts readily available throughout the country for their dissemination.

One important unanswered question about the impact of tourism concerns its ecological effects. The exploitation of Spanish, French, Italian, Greek, and other Mediterranean beaches for tourist developments has often had a ruinous effect on the coastal ecology. It remains to be seen if this will occur in Tunisia, but the slight attention paid to environmental issues as hotels have sprung up suggests it is a distinct possibility. Despite these drawbacks, the success of tourism in securing desperately needed foreign revenue ensures its continuation as a vitally important facet of the Tunisian economy. By exposing Tunisians to modern alternatives to traditional lifestyles, it serves as one of many catalysts for social change. Over the long run, however, its greatest contribution may well lie in the lines of communication it has opened between Tunisia and the West, facilitating the prospects for dialogue and better mutual understanding.

NOTES

1. The urban growth rate between 1975 and 1980 has been estimated at 3.8 percent, well above the national average. In contrast, rural growth was about 1 percent, well below the average and a confirmation of the rural exodus.

2. Overseas donors accounted for 36 percent of the total funding of the Fifth Five-Year Plan (1977–1981) and a similarly high proportion of the sixth plan. Mzali could not afford to ignore donor agencies' demands, despite his awareness of their probable political and social repercussions.

11

Independent Tunisia's Political Culture

Habib Bourguiba has dominated the politics of independent Tunisia. Since 1957, the country has had no other head of state, and, although a number of prime ministers with various official policies have succeeded one another, the president has remained. His tenure has provided a measure of continuity uncommon in Third World politics but has also created a dangerous situation in which the highest echelons of power have lost touch with critical segments of the population.

THE ROLE OF THE PARTY

One reason for Bourguiba's political longevity is his mastery of a highly organized mass political movement that did not break up after winning the battle for independence but was instead channeled in new directions by the people who had always led it. The pyramidal structure devised by the nationalists in the 1930s has remained the framework of the party to the present, allowing for strong central control of its apparatus at every level. Several local cells, organized geographically or professionally, form a *circonscription*. A Coordinating Committee oversees the operations of circonscriptions in each governorate. At periodic party congresses, locally selected delegates choose a Central Committee to formulate party policies. A Political Bureau (the party's executive board) is drawn from the Central Committee. The principal officers of the party are the secretary general; the director, who manages day-to-day party business; and, at the apex of the pyramid, the president, a post only Bourguiba has held and to which he received a lifetime appointment in 1974.

Bourguiba and his associates have worked assiduously and, with a few rare exceptions, successfully to maintain undisputed control of

147

the party. As his own contemporaries on the Political Bureau died or quarreled with him, he engineered their replacement by younger persons with less influence and no well-developed bases of power. To curb the Political Bureau further, Bourguiba orchestrated frequent reshufflings. In the mid-1970s, the party abandoned the practice of having the Central Committee elect the Political Bureau. Instead, Bourguiba, in his capacity as party president, chose the entire body, guaranteeing its loyalty to him.

Party membership after World War II approached 200,000, although not all members qualified as militants or active participants in the nationalist struggle. By the late 1950s, however, the party's ranks had almost tripled. Prior to independence, the Neo-Dustur attracted new adherents as it pushed France toward ending the protectorate. After 1956, the need to prove allegiance to the party to obtain good government jobs further swelled its rolls. From an artificial high in the late 1950s, membership steadied at around 300,000 in the next decade. Since then, it has risen with population growth, standing now at about half a million.

The rapid increase in the number of party members in the first years of independence meant that there were often shortages of trained local leaders to manage new or enlarged cells, a difficulty compounded by the government's policy of rewarding veteran Neo-Dusturians with jobs in the bureaucracy. A more serious problem was the loss of purpose many militants experienced after 1956, leading to a certain stagnation within the party. Bourguiba and his colleagues understood that their success in modernizing Tunisian society depended on their ability to shift the party's emphasis from anticolonial activities to mobilizing support for reforms. Particularly at the lower echelons, however, many activists found it more difficult to grasp the party's new plans than they had the simpler and more straightforward struggle against the French. The new Neo-Dustur goals required a more sophisticated leadership than the heads of many cells could provide.

Even party leaders frequently preferred to rest on their accomplishments in the nationalist era rather than to address thorny contemporary issues. This attitude, encouraged by the continuing prominence in the party of people associated with its heroic past, convinced many Tunisian youths that the Neo-Dustur had little interest in, or even awareness of, the difficulties peculiar to their generation. Well-educated young men and women entered government service or took positions in parastatal industries only to find their advancement blocked by the presence of individuals who owed their jobs not to their talents but to their long affiliation with the Neo-Dustur.

Although the party and the state remained theoretically distinct, indications that the line between them was blurry were not long in appearing. A party reorganization in 1958 resulted in a highly centralized structure whose components neatly corresponded with regional and local government units. Several years later, party and state were still more closely linked when regional government officials were assigned responsibility for party management in their areas and regional party committees were integrated into existing regional government agencies. Although these steps helped party leaders mobilize support for the government, the increasing centralization made it more difficult for local members to influence party policy-making. Such circumstances provided an early stimulus for rank-and-file complaints about the absence of democracy in the party. The adoption of socialist principles, formalized at the 1964 party congress, was in part an attempt to restore the enthusiasm of many party members, especially the young.

THE POWER OF THE PRESIDENCY

Amin Bey, Tunisia's septuagenarian head of state in 1956, hardly provided the appropriate image for the dynamic new society the Neo-Dustur envisioned. He represented an outmoded political order, and Bourguiba, whose power derived from his leadership of a mass popular movement, determined to end this antiquated arrangement: He deposed Amin in 1957. The unwillingness of the monarchs (with the possible exception of Munsif) to support Tunisian nationalism to preserve the few vestiges of authority that the French had left them had created a gulf between the royal family and the Neo-Dusturians. As president of the the new Republic of Tunisia, however, Bourguiba relegated the assembly he had fought so long to establish to a secondary role, introducing many of his most important early social, economic, and political reforms through executive decrees only later ratified by the assembly.

Bourguiba knew that the abolition of the beylicate would strike a responsive chord in the camp of Ben Yusuf and the other extreme nationalists. Ben Yusuf's stress on Tunisia's Arab identity, his proclivity for Marxism and revolutionary change, and his distrust of the West starkly contrasted with the Mediterranean orientation and gradualism of Bourguiba. The Yusufist movement alarmed Bourguiba, and, although he and his allies never really lost control, his rival's popularity shook Bourguiba's faith in his country's people. He was convinced that the Tunisians lacked the political sophistication to evaluate wisely options confronting them. In the president's paternalistic view, a strong hand was needed to smoothly guide the masses toward progressive goals and prevent them from succumbing to harmful rhetoric. Although the possibility of an organized challenge to the new regime hovered in the background until Ben Yusuf's mysterious assassination in Cairo in 1961, Bourguiba slowly and steadily consolidated power.

The constitution promulgated in 1959 enshrined the concept of a strong chief executive and a weak legislature. Among its provisions were articles making government ministers directly responsible to the president; permitting him to rule by decree when the assembly was not in session; and giving preference to legislation he proposed. For most ordinary Tunisians, Bourguiba embodied the state. This perfectly suited the Neo-Dustur leaders, who hoped that personal respect for Bourguiba would translate into respect for the policies of the new government. All important political decisions were taken in the president's office. The National Assembly capped Bourguiba's powers by making him president for life in 1974.

Partly in response to the Ben Yusuf affair, Bourguiba decided early on to brook no personal competitors and permit no rival ideologies. The resulting uniformity would, he believed, ease the processes of development and transformation by keeping dissent to a minimum. His extensive governmental powers and his control over the Neo-Dustur enabled him to remove critics from the political arena and build a classic single-party state. In keeping with his characteristic moderation, however, the president customarily restored those with whom he had fallen out to significant positions in the party or the government after a sobering stay in the political wilderness. (Ben Salah's appointment as minister of planning in 1961, despite his attacks on the government while he headed the UGTT, is a good example.) The ease with which he imposed these punishments underscored Bourguiba's might, and the practice of reintegrating those who had strayed from the proper path prevented the emergence of an organized, coordinated opposition for many years.

Thus, the first challenge to Bourguiba and the Neo-Dustur was also the last for a decade and a half. The political counterculture of the 1960s was unimpressive. The only organization besides the Neo-Dustur was the small Tunisian Communist party. Although allowing the party to survive, the government so severely restricted its activities that it was rendered impotent.

Since the late 1960s, Bourguiba has experienced several periods of ill health, during some of which his physical and mental faculties seem to have been temporarily impaired. These ailments prompted a constitutional amendment in 1975 stipulating that the prime minister succeed to the presidency on the death of the incumbent. Uncertainty about the nature of the post-Bourguiba state is a critical concern in contemporary Tunisia, especially as the president has made few efforts to groom potential successors during his decades in power. Since 1956, Tunisian politicians have operated in Bourguiba's shadow. Although none enjoys the prestige of the "Supreme Combattant" (as Bourguiba is known for his role in the nationalist struggle and in bringing about social change), his earlier exploits, many of which have assumed mythic proportions, carry less weight than they once did for people mostly born after 1956 and having no awareness of a political or social situation other than the present one. Beginning in the deteriorating economic circumstances of the 1970s, criticisms of the regime's autocracy and demands for greater participation in the political process increased, but the president rejected appeals to liberalize the political system. This lack of responsiveness, coupled with serious economic problems, spawned opposition groups spanning the political spectrum from the Left to the Right. Only in the 1980s did some loosening occur, although not enough to satisfy PSD critics.

THE OPPOSITION

The political career of Ahmad Ben Salah, widely regarded in the 1960s as Bourguiba's heir apparent, disintegrated with the government's renunciation of his efforts to expand collectivized agriculture. Removed from office and blamed for all the shortcomings of economic planning, Ben Salah went to prison in 1969. He escaped in 1973, fled the country, and formed the Mouvement d'Unité Populaire (MUP), a socialist party advocating many of the same programs he had attempted to implement as planning minister. Most of Ben Salah's supporters were exiled Tunisian intellectuals, and the MUP had little impact on Tunisian politics.

The virtually unlimited power Ben Salah had exercised during much of his tenure in the Planning Ministry had shocked many of the nation's political elites. Even some individuals deeply committed to PSD traditions expressed their regret at how easily Bourguiba had elevated Ben Salah to his position without regard for opposing sentiments. They reasoned that the only way to prevent a similar and perhaps even more costly error in the future was to impose institutional restraints on the aging Bourguiba's enormous and unchecked powers. The president's failing health seemed to reinforce the need for such steps.

Ahmad Mistiri had been one of several influential young party members to resign government appointments in protest over PSD economic policies in the 1960s. After Ben Salah's fall and his own rehabilitation, Mistiri began a campaign to democratize certain party procedures. Pledging to work for new rules that would allow the party congress to choose the Political Bureau, Mistiri won election to the PSD Central Committee in 1971. In his pursuit of reforms he ran afoul of Bourguiba, who had him dismissed from the party as a disruptive element. To halt any further drift toward liberalism a reinvigorated Bourguiba took personal command of the party at its 1974 congress, a move symbolized by his assumption of the right to appoint the entire Political Bureau. This hard-line resulted in a purge of PSD liberals who naturally looked to Mistiri for leadership. After the 1978 general strike, Mistiri tried to organize a formal political party, the Mouvement des Démocrates Sociales (MDS), but the government thwarted his efforts.

Another contributor to the opposition crystallizing in the 1970s was Muhammad Masmudi. As foreign minister in 1974, Masmudi negotiated a Libyan-Tunisian merger that he claimed would alleviate some of Tunisia's economic woes by providing jobs in Libya for unemployed Tunisians and giving the Tunisian government access to Libyan financial resources. Bourguiba initially accepted the idea but later withdrew his support and ejected Masmudi from both the government and the PSD. The exminister did not create a formal political organization, but his criticisms of the regime and his good relations with revolutionary Libya made him an important focal point for anti-Bourguibist activists.

After the Black Thursday demonstrations the government could no longer ignore the national malaise. The riots not only brought economic grievances to the forefront but also paved the way for changes in the political sphere as many responsible Dusturians concluded that the government faced a choice between the complete repression of the opposition and the introduction of at least some liberal reforms to satisfy its critics. An indication of the possibly dire consequences of failing to address the causes of popular discontent appeared on the second anniversary of Black Thursday when dissidents, allegedly trained in Libya, seized the southern city of Gafsa, holding it for several hours before Tunisian armed forces retook it and captured most of them.

Antigovernment sentiment ran deeper in the economically depressed south than elsewhere in the country because of its high unemployment and the massive migration of its young men to the cities or abroad in search of jobs. Taking their cue from government officials themselves, the foreign investors who had flocked to Tunisia in the 1970s had largely ignored the south, preferring the Sahil and the Tunis area which had better educated work forces and easier access to European markets. The south, still heavily dependent on the phosphate industry, suffered further as the world market price for the mineral declined. The susceptibility of disgruntled citizens to antiregime propaganda and the unprecedented extremism of the Gafsa incident raised the alarming spectre of a popular uprising fueled by both internal and external opponents of the regime. It should be noted, however, that all the opposition leaders, including Masmudi, who continued to maintain close ties with Libya, condemned the Gafsa attack.

When Prime Minister Nuwaira died a few months later, his more liberally inclined successor, Muhammad Mzali, inaugurated an "open government" that made some efforts to heal the rift between the regime and its critics. Mzali freed many UGTT leaders imprisoned since 1978 and allowed Ashur to resume his position as secretary general of the union. He also reintegrated Mistiri and his supporters into the PSD and, in a political first, authorized them to publish an opposition newspaper. The 1981 PSD congress went still further, endorsing the concept of a multiparty system provided that new political organizations did not challenge Bourguiba personally, did not rely on support from outside the country, and did not advocate class struggle or sectarianism. The Mouvement des Démocrates Sociales won formal recognition as a party only late in 1983, although as the head of an informally constituted "loyal opposition" within the PSD, Mistiri benefited from the new regulations from the outset. The Communist party also took immediate advantage of them to acquire full legal status, and the MUP-2, a moderate splinter group from Ben Salah's MUP, was permitted to participate in the political process in 1983.

Despite party conservatives' bids to stifle these reforms, Mzali managed to retain Bourguiba's confidence. But the outbreak of the most serious rioting since independence in January 1984—over the removal of government subsidies from several basic commodities— badly shook his government. Bourguiba, adopting a benevolent and paternal image, immediately ordered the price hikes rescinded. By renouncing his prime minister's unpopular action, Bourguiba promoted the belief that Mzali bore sole responsibility for the increases, although Tunisia's international creditors had left him with few options. This act undermined Mzali's image and opened him to attacks by the outraged public as well as by PSD hard-liners who blamed the disorders on Mzali's liberal policies. Nevertheless, Bourguiba did not withdraw his support for the prime minister. Somewhat chastened and very much indebted to the president, Mzali remained in office, but his critics' intense attacks made it difficult for him to continue his liberal policies.

After the bread riots, senior military officers made a point of expressing their displeasure at the government's repeated use of the armed forces to suppress dissent and quell civil disorders, tasks both they and their troops found extremely distasteful. As disenchantment with the regime increased in the late 1970s, the military budget skyrocketed, but many of these funds went toward preparing the army to cope with civil disorders rather than its primary function of national defense, another irritant to the professional officers. In view of Bourguiba's firm and consistent discouragement of any military involvement in the political arena, this criticism was something of a new departure. Since most Tunisian soldiers came from class backgrounds similar to the rioters' and experienced many of the same socioeconomic ills, the officers' observations, though not intended to threaten the government directly, did carry grave implications for the politicians to contemplate before allowing another confrontation between the armed forces and civilians.

In addition to his secular adversaries, Mzali also had to contend with an opposition movement rooted in Islam. The Neo-Dustur's long-standing disdain for the religious establishment stemmed from the ulama's ineffectiveness in opposing colonialism. The successful postindependence campaign to subordinate Islamic institutions to the state antagonized Muslim traditionalists, as did many of the social and economic reforms of the 1960s. They viewed the PSD's innovations as un-Islamic and destructive to cherished cultural values, but they lacked the political leverage to prevent them.

The ouster of Ben Salah and his supporters in 1969, followed by the purge of PSD liberals five years later, removed from the political scene the most outspoken proponents of societal restructuring and cleared the way for a dramatic increase in the influence of more conservative elements, including religious traditionalists. The government tried to forestall the emergence of a radical Arabo-Islamic movement by appearing to link itself more closely to traditional Islamic institutions and attempting to boost the prestige of the state-controlled ulama. But this tactical exploitation of religion only further incensed those who wished to build a society based on Islamic principles.

The Mouvement de Tendance Islamique (MTI), established by Rashid Ghannushi early in the 1970s, achieved greater visibility than other groups similarly committed to fostering an Islamic way of life in Tunisia. The MTI criticized the westernized elite's fascination with imported and often inappropriate ideologies and condemned the decline of traditional values, which it blamed on the PSD's emphasis on social change. In articles and public sermons, Ghannushi asserted that Tunisian reliance on a Western model of economic development contingent on the massive infusion of international capital would not only fail but would bring with it the corruption and materialism that he saw as inevitable byproducts of such a system. To manifest their rejection of foreign influences, Ghannushi urged his followers to wear traditional clothing and publicly comport themselves in a fashion consonant with Islamic criteria. Although specific conditions within Tunisia had given rise to the MTI, the movement constituted part of a broad trend discernible throughout the Middle East and North Africa. In the malaise occasioned by the catastrophic Arab defeat in the June 1967 war with Israel, many Arabs had begun to question the validity of (the largely alien) political, social, and economic structures that had failed to meet the most important challenges they had faced since independence. Despite Tunisia's minimal involvement in the events of 1967, the founders of the MTI shared this uneasiness and acted in part as a result of it.

As dissatisfaction with the Nuwaira government increased, the MTI strove to acquaint Tunisians with Islamic alternatives to Western notions, particularly targeting secondary-school students. The organization grew significantly in the last half of the 1970s, becoming more politicized at the same time. Many educated young men and women of the lower and middle classes, deprived of opportunity in the crisis-ridden economy and finding channels of protest closed by a regime that repressed dissent, abandoned what they saw as the bankrupt philosophies of Tunisia's westernized leaders and formed the bulk of the MTI's new recruits. Once again, an external factor enhanced the appeal of the MTI. The Iranian Revolution, by proving that a popular Islamic movement could overpower even a well-entrenched secular dictatorship, gave renewed inspiration to efforts to instill Tunisian society with a more Islamic orientation.

MTI activism led to a ban on its journal in 1979 and Ghannushi's imprisonment in 1981. Even Prime Minister Mzali's open government refused to allow the participation in the political process of an association so critical of the fundamental underpinnings of the Tunisian state. The PSD reached its 1981 decision to exclude groups advocating sectarianism from the multiparty experiment with the MTI in mind. It also rejected an MTI request for legalization as a political party in 1984, charging that the group's leaders had provoked the January bread riots. The riots did epitomize MTI grievances concerning government dependence on outside support and lack of concern for Tunisians' welfare, and many MTI members and sympathizers did take part in the disorders. But the MTI had not engineered them, and militants arrested after the riots were freed, along with Ghannushi, in mid-1984. Although the shaky Mzali government has continued to withhold legal recognition as a party from the MTI, the group has kept up its demand for legalization, expressing a willingness to work within the existing system if permitted to do so.

12

Foreign Relations

THE MAGHRIB

Tunisia's constitution advocates Maghrib unity, but the widely divergent political and economic systems of Morocco, Algeria, Libya, and Tunisia have made this goal difficult to attain. Since 1956 relations between Tunisia and its North African neighbors have fluctuated between close, mutually beneficial political and economic alliances and hostile encounters verging on war.

For centuries, Tunisians have regarded relations with their more populous and usually more powerful western neighbor, Algeria, as particularly important. The revolution against French control begun by the Algerian Front de Libération Nationale (FLN) in 1954 ended only in 1962. After 1956, the fighting in Algeria put Tunisian officials in a diplomatic dilemma. In view of their own recently completed independence struggle, they could hardly fail to support the Algerian rebels, nor did they wish to. However, Tunisia had to remain on reasonably good terms with France, which continued to supply economic and technical assistance after the termination of the protectorate. The presence in Tunisia of key FLN exiles complicated relations with France, as did the large number of Algerian refugees on the Tunisian side of the frontier. The 25,000 FLN soldiers operating from sanctuaries on Tunisian soil, however, created the greatest problem. French forces built an electrified border fence, the Morice Line, to prevent FLN incursions from Tunisia, and, in 1958, French planes attacked the Tunisian village of Saqiyat Sidi Yusuf, causing extensive property damage and many casualties.

Such Tunisian sacrifices on behalf of the Algerian Revolution might have produced a strong fraternal bond except that crucial Tunisian and Algerian interests did not always coincide. In 1961, while France still controlled Algeria, Tunisia unsuccessfully sought recognition of its claims to oil-producing areas of the Algerian Sahara. The Algerian nationalists resented this attempt to secure economic

157

gains at their country's expense, and relations deteriorated. They declined further when Tunisia turned toward a capitalist form of development in the 1970s, much to the disgust of Algeria's President Houari Boumedienne, a prominent champion of socialism. Aside from a few mutually profitable economic links, contacts between the two countries remained minimal and were characterized by mistrust throughout the 1960s and 1970s.

Boumedienne's death in 1979 led to a change in Tunisian-Algerian relations. The new president, Shadli Ben Jadid, inaugurated a less ideological, more pragmatic approach to foreign policy. Tensions with Tunisia eased, and the number of cooperative projects, including an oil pipeline from Algeria to Sicily across Tunisia, increased. In 1983, the two countries signed an accord laying the groundwork for a Maghrib union broadly patterned on the European Economic Community and the Gulf Co-operation Council. They invited other North African states to adhere to the treaty, but only Mauritania accepted. The obvious advantages of attaching Tunisia's faltering economy to the oil-rich one of Algeria provided a strong stimulus for improved relations. Moreover, the alliance with Algeria gave Tunisia a valuable counterweight in its frequently stormy dealings with another powerful neighbor, Libya.

Tunisian dealings with the Libyan monarchy had been free of serious problems. Libya's booming economy and small population made it a well-paying source of jobs for thousands of unemployed Tunisian workers. Colonel Qaddafi's 1969 coup had no affect on labor migration, and, for a time, good relations continued. The new Libyan leader's militant insistence on Arab unity, however, eventually soured contacts. Bourguiba disliked Qaddafi's impetuosity. He did not oppose the principle of unity but believed it should be pursued slowly and cautiously. The young soldier, on the other hand, regarded the aging politician as hopelessly mired in the past. In 1974, with Bourguiba in ill health and his hold over the party apparatus weak, Tunisian Foreign Minister Masmudi arranged a merger between Libya and Tunisia. Bourguiba initially consented but later renounced the plan and removed Masmudi from office. Qaddafi blamed the policy reversal on Tunisia's ties with Western European and U.S. enemies of Arab unity. Harshly criticizing Bourguiba, Qaddafi vowed to support the Tunisian opposition, beginning an era of Libyan meddling in Tunisian domestic politics.

Links between Libya and Tunisian dissidents grew stronger as the political and economic situation in Tunisia worsened. Because many Tunisian workers in Libya came from the particularly depressed south, they were especially receptive to antiregime propaganda, which they carried across the border on their visits home. Libyan authorities occasionally rounded up illegal Tunisian immigrants, of whom there were many, and threatened them with imprisonment or deportation unless they agreed to participate in subversive activities, including training as guerrillas. In addition to ordinary workers, some prominent critics of the PSD also established contacts with Libyan officials and exiled Tunisian opponents of the government. For example, the president of the increasingly discontented UGTT, Habib Ashur, met with Masmudi during a visit to Libya to set up a branch of the union for Tunisian workers there in the late 1970s.

Qaddafi's antagonism toward Bourguiba culminated in the January 1980 attack on Gafsa by Tunisians trained in Libya.[1] Outraged at this attempt to undermine his government, Bourguiba severed relations with Libya. Qaddafi retaliated by deporting more than 10,000 Tunisian workers. Holding the government responsible for the loss of their lucrative jobs abroad and unable to find employment at home, these returned workers added to the political and economic woes of a regime grappling with already critical problems. Ongoing Libyan efforts to destabilize the Tunisian government enabled PSD officials to place the blame for all their domestic problems at Qaddafi's doorstep. Thus, Libyan instigators were accused of precipitating the 1984 bread riots. Although Libya undeniably took advantage of those disorders to spread discontent with the government, popular resentment with PSD economic policies was sufficiently strong to trigger the disturbances without prompting from Libya. Tunisian officials also charged Qaddafi with deliberately fomenting additional troubles for their regime by deporting another large contingent of Tunisian workers in 1985. By then, however, Libya's oil-based economy had encountered serious difficulties, and many of its foreign workers were, in fact, no longer needed.

Libyan antipathy toward Tunisia did much to foster the improved relations between Tunisia and Algeria that ultimately led to their 1983 accord on economic and political cooperation. Qaddafi, who had fallen out with the Algerians on several major issues, viewed that treaty as an attempt to isolate Libya. To counter this possibility, he signed a similar pact with King Hassan of Morocco in early 1984. Although Morocco and Libya pursued widely divergent policies on most matters, Hassan had long been at odds with Algeria, whereas Moroccan-Tunisan relations had rarely been more than lukewarm.

Although Morocco was the North African state with which Tunisia had the most in common philosophically and ideologically, the two frequently disagreed on matters of both substance and style. Just as he later questioned Qaddafi's drive to broaden Libyan hegemony through the concept of Arab unity, Bourguiba did not accept at face value the idea of a Greater Morocco expounded even before independence by many Moroccan nationalists and the monarchy. In 1960, he criticized Moroccan claims to Mauritania, calling instead for the complete independence of the former French West African territory.

In a more recent example of the Greater Morocco notion, the kingdom has, since 1975, fought a protracted guerrilla war with the Polisario (the Popular Front for the Liberation of Saguia el-Hamra and Rio de Oro). This liberation movement has worked to thwart Moroccan attempts to impose its control over the Western Sahara (formerly the colony of Spanish Sahara). From the beginning, Tunisia had misgivings about the validity of Morocco's claim and King Hassan's unwillingness to allow the Western Saharans a voice in determining their future. Moreover, it saw no point in antagonizing Polisario's two most vigorous supporters—who also happened to be neighbors with whom it was not on the best of terms—Algeria and Libya. Aside from encouraging negotiations between Morocco and backers of the Polisario, Tunisia has carefully refrained from any direct involvement in the dispute. However, attitudes about Morocco and Polisario were clearly determining factors in the political realignments in the Maghrib in 1983 and 1984 (Algeria, Tunisia, and Mauritania, on one hand; Morocco and Libya, on the other).

THE EASTERN ARAB WORLD

Egypt's president Gamal Abdel Nasser was by far the most prominent figure in the Arab world when Tunisia gained its independence. Bourguiba and the Egyptian leader strongly disagreed over many fundamental issues and never worked well together. Bourguiba did not share Nasser's enthusiasm for Arab unity, preferring to focus on less broadly defined questions more susceptible to immediate resolution. Nor did he approve of Nasser's confrontation politics with Israel. He believed the Tunisian case had amply demonstrated that the moderate, step-by-step approach of "Bourguibism" achieved better results in the long run. Bourguiba's most outspoken critic, Salah Ben Yusuf, frequently expressed his admiration for the Egyptian president and support for his Arab nationalist views, further souring the Neo-Dustur leader on Nasser. As a protest of Nasser's domination of the Arab League, Tunisia did not join the organization until 1958; for several years thereafter it participated only minimally in its affairs. Tunisia joined the United Nations immediately, however. By thus distancing himself from his fellow Arabs while maintaining close ties with France, Bourguiba left himself open to the charge that he was more anxious to remain in the good graces of the West than to do battle with the most critical issues facing the Arabo-Islamic world, including that of Palestine.

The official Tunisian position on Palestine perfectly reflected Bourguibist principles. It acknowledged the justice of the Palestinian cause but questioned the tactics Arab leaders used to assist the Palestinians. In the course of a visit to the Middle East in 1965, Bourguiba urged the Palestinians to adopt the same step-by-step method that the Neo-Dustur had successfully used in its independence struggle. As a specific opening maneuver, he suggested that their leaders accept the provisions of the 1947 UN partition plan for Palestine. Israel would almost certainly reject this overture, he went on, thereby assuming an obstructionist role and winning international sympathy for the Palestinians' willingness to compromise. The recently created Palestine Liberation Organization (PLO), then very much under Egyptian control, ridiculed Bourguiba's ideas, accused him of defeatism, and began a steady propaganda barrage in which Nasser joined. So vehement were the attacks on Bourguiba in the Palestinian and Egyptian media that Tunisia severed relations with Egypt in the following year.

Israel's stunning defeat of Egypt, Syria, and Jordan in June 1967 seemed to bear out Bourguiba's criticisms of Arab policy on Palestine. But events in Tunisia in the weeks surrounding the war revealed a significant gap between the thinking of the ruling elite and the rest of the populace on this emotionally charged issue.[2] In common with Arabs everywhere, Tunisians saw the June War as both a humiliating disaster and a positive proof of the expansionist aims of Zionism. In their anger, they rejected moderation as an appropriate response. A wave of demonstrations in support of Nasser and pan-Arabism swept the country, as did acts of anti-Semitism against Tunisia's small Jewish community, which had traditionally enjoyed good relations with its Muslim neighbors. The spontaneity and vigor of this support for the Palestinians prompted Bourguiba to act more in harmony with popular opinion. In a show of Arab fraternity, a few Tunisian military units were even dispatched to the front, but, owing to the shortness of the war, never saw action.

The restoration of diplomatic ties with Egypt symbolized the improvement of Tunisian relations with the Arab East after the war. Bourguiba stressed the dangers of renewed full-scale war in the Middle East, but even he agreed with the widespread sentiment that, under the circumstances, armed struggle was the only option available to the Palestinians. The upswing in guerrilla activities after the June War created new tensions between the revitalized PLO and the governments from whose territory its commandos operated. Jordan's King Hussain particularly worried about the implications for himself and his country of nourishing the Palestinian revolution. In September 1970, the king launched a war to drive the PLO from Jordan. Characteristically, Bourguiba urged moderation on both sides. Tunisian Prime Minister Badi Ladgham played an important role in mediations that helped end the fighting, although not before it had badly scarred all the parties.

The death of President Nasser in 1970 removed the last obstacle to Tunisia's participating more extensively in Middle Eastern affairs. Bourguiba's own ill health in the early years of the decade enabled subordinates more strongly attracted to Arabism than the president himself to influence foreign policy. As a result, Tunisia's identification with the Arabo-Islamic world was enhanced. Muhammad Masmudi, the foreign minister from 1970 until his ouster over the proposed Libyan merger in 1974, was primarily responsible for implementing the new policy. His reputation as an Arab nationalist enabled him to mend fences with Middle Eastern leaders still skeptical of Tunisia's commitment to Arabism and to initiate important new contacts throughout the Arab world. Increased Tunisian interest in the Arab East brought with it heightened enthusiasm for many Arab and Islamic themes previously receiving little attention. It was no coincidence that Islamic organizations, some of which later became centers of opposition to the government, first began to take shape at this time.

Egyptian President Anwar Sadat's visit to Jerusalem in 1977 set in motion an unexpected chain of events that added to Tunisian prominence in Arab circles. The 1979 Egyptian-Israeli Peace Treaty led to Egypt's ostracism from the Arab world. The Arab League, whose offices had been in Cairo since 1945, expressed its displeasure by transferring them to Tunis. Tunisians filled key posts in the league's bureaucracy, including that of secretary general, giving their country a stronger voice in Arab affairs than ever before. When the Israeli siege of Beirut in summer 1982 forced the PLO to withdraw from that city, its leaders also selected Tunis as their new headquarters.

An extremely pragmatic benefit of Tunisia's warmer relationship with the Arab East was an increase in economic aid, in the form of both investments and grants, from the oil-producing states. Tunisia joined the Organization of Arab Petroleum Exporting Countries (OAPEC) in 1982, more to underscore its affinity with other Arab states than for reasons stemming from the production or marketing of oil. Prior to the 1980s, Arab sources accounted for about 20 percent of Tunisia's total foreign aid. In the Sixth Five-Year Plan (1982–1986), their share rose to almost one-third. Another economic benefit of good relations with the Arab East was the opportunity afforded to Tunisians for employment in the Arabian peninsula. Salaries there were often better than those earned by workers in Europe, and the social discomfort was less than that frequently experienced by guest workers in the West. The transfer of the PLO bureaucracy led to Tunisia's becoming more directly enmeshed in the Arab-Israeli conflict than ever before. In 1985, Israeli jets bombed a Palestinian encampment near Tunis as part of an escalating campaign of terrorist attacks and counterattacks involving Israelis, Palestinians, and other Arabs throughout the Middle East and North Africa. Although Tunisians were shaken by this demonstration of the Israelis' ability to carry out offensive operations on their own soil, the raid resulted in a stiffening of anti-Israeli sentiment and an increase in public support for the government's assistance to the PLO.

EUROPE

Better Tunisian relations with the Arab world in the 1970s and 1980s supplemented, rather than replaced, long-established ties with the West. France has provided the primary point of contact with the West, but dealings with the former colonizer have not always been friendly. For many years after independence, the Tunisian government employed French teachers and technical experts to fill important posts for which there were not enough qualified Tunisians. Although this form of ongoing French presence was appreciated, the continued stationing of even a small number of French troops on Tunisian soil after 1956 provided an irritant to Franco-Tunisian relations, particularly in light of the French army's mission to suppress the Algerian Revolution.

Tunisia restricted the movement of French forces remaining in the country following the 1958 bombing of the Tunisian border village of Saqiyat Sidi Yusuf. Shortly thereafter, France agreed to limit its troops to a few isolated posts in the Sahara and its large naval base at Bizerte. Tunisians chafed at the extensive operations at the Bizerte installation. When France expanded its facilities there in 1961, despite persistent Tunisian objections, Bourguiba dug in and demanded the base's evacuation. He knew, however, that France, facing the prospect of losing its many military and naval positions in Algeria, would not abandon Bizerte without a fight. Consequently, the Neo-Dustur mobilized a cadre of militants, many of them veterans of the short-lived guerrilla fighting before independence, to blockade the base and launch a series of commando raids. France responded by dropping paratroopers to reinforce the garrison. In the ensuing combat, the

French captured the road and railway linking Bizerte to Tunis, as well as large parts of the city itself. Most of the small Tunisian army was in the south, attempting to gain control over areas still occupied by France, and could provide little support in the battle for Bizerte. The inadequately armed and trained civilians and paramilitary units defending the city sustained thousands of casualties.

Tunisia quickly brought the Bizerte issue before the United Nations. The international organization partially supported the Tunisian position by calling upon France to withdraw immediately within the confines of its bases, but it urged bilateral negotiations to determine the base's ultimate fate. France ignored the UN stance and continued to occupy Bizerte for several weeks. It also postponed discussions over the final disposition of the base until after the Algerian War had ended in the following summer. France feared that the FLN might seize upon negotiations over Bizerte as a precedent for demanding the evacuation of the even larger French naval base at Mars al-Kabir, west of Oran, as a condition for ending the war. France finally turned the Bizerte base over to Tunisian naval authorities in late 1963.

These events represented an enormous victory for Bourguiba within Tunisia. Tunisians reveled in the demonstration that their country had come of age and proved itself able to hold its own against external pressures, even when they came from the once dreaded colonial power. The Bizerte Affair also underscored the great personal popularity of the president. At this early stage of independence, Tunisians still almost universally looked upon Bourguiba as a father figure and their greatest national hero. Despite the heavy loss of life in the confrontation, neither the Tunisian people nor the Neo-Dustur ever wavered in their support of Bourguiba.

Internationally, however, Tunisian handling of the Bizerte matter caused difficulties. The obviously important and generally beneficial relationship with France collapsed, and other nations also placed Tunisia at arm's length. Until 1961, Bourguiba's moderate, essentially pro-Western philosophy had appealed to European leaders, who considered him an Afro-Asian statesman with whom they could cooperate. They feared that his actions at Bizerte marked a permanent shift away from traditional Bourguibist principles, not merely a temporary tactic. Given the Cold War mentality of the time, many Westerners interpreted Tunisia's militant demands for the evacuation of Bizerte not in terms of national pride but rather as proof of the growth of Soviet meddling and influence in Africa in general and, in tandem with the Algerian Revolution, in the Maghrib in particular. Tunisian relations with the Communist world were, in fact, warmer

Avenue Habib Bourguiba, the main street of modern Tunis. (Photo by author)

during and immediately after the Bizerte crisis than at any time before or since, although Moscow exercised no control over Tunis. Even those Western leaders who understood the true sources of Tunisian anger over the Bizerte base regretted the loss of so potentially important a Cold War stronghold in the hotly contested arena of Africa and the Middle East.

Bourguiba took advantage of the anti-French sentiments the Bizerte Affair generated to expropriate colon land in 1964. Nevertheless, historical, geographical, and linguistic circumstances made it inevitable that Franco-Tunisian relations would take a favorable turn after a cooling-off period had demonstrated that no fundamental reorientation in Tunisian politics had occurred. In 1969, France helped Tunisia attain associate membership in the European Economic Community, and Tunisia actively sought better relations with France as it began to experiment with a more open economy in the 1970s. Since then contacts have centered on economic matters, most notably development aid, investments, and military assistance. Arabization has decreased the need for French-speaking teachers, but French technical help in agricultural, public-works, and public-health projects has been substantial. French firms' connections with Tunisia, some of which predate the protectorate, have kept France the primary supplier of Tunisian imports, even during times of political tensions. France also provides the bulk of Tunisia's military materiel and much of the advanced training for its armed forces.

Although Paris and Tunis have not always agreed on specific policy decisions, France has consistently characterized the political situation in Tunisia as preferable to any probable alternatives. France made the strength of its commitment to the Bourguiba regime clear in the aftermath of the Gafsa raid by rushing additional military equipment to Tunisia along with a promise of military intervention if necessary to guarantee the integrity of the country's frontiers.

Business has also dominated Tunisia's postindependence dealings with other Western European states, although none of those nations has approached France in terms of the magnitude or intensity of its contacts with Tunisia. In addition to attracting Western European investors, Tunisia has benefited from economic aid contributed especially by West Germany and the Scandinavian countries, as well as from the stream of European tourists. Tunisia has also cultivated European markets for its products and its excess labor force. Italy has been the major continental consumer of Tunisian goods, but during the 1980s, EEC import restrictions and the entry into the Common Market of southern European countries producing goods similar to Tunisia's have reduced the volume of exports across the Mediterranean.

THE UNITED STATES

Despite minimal private U.S. investments in Tunisia, the United States has been the largest single supplier of aid to the country, providing more than $1 billion in the three decades since independence. U.S. assistance was intended to foster economic development and contribute to the stability of a nation whose policies, with a few notable exceptions, have generally accorded with those of the United States. Beyond this confluence of views on matters of mutual importance, Tunisia's location beside the narrow sealanes of the central Mediterranean is of great strategic value to the Western alliance in general and to the U.S. Sixth Fleet in particular. Initially, development aid constituted the largest portion of U.S. assistance. Since the late 1970s, however, military aid has risen in prominence. In 1984, military sales and grants to Tunisia exceeded $100 million, compared with less than $13 million in economic assistance. This contrasts with an annual total aid commitment of roughly $50 million at the end of the 1970s, less than half of which was earmarked for the armed forces.[3]

The U.S. decision to emphasize military aid came in response to Tunisian government claims that its small armed forces needed more and better equipment to protect the country from neighbors intent on meddling in its domestic politics. U.S. officials, who already considered Libya a primary source of instability and anti-Western sentiment throughout the Middle East and Africa, were anxious to help friendly governments contain Qaddafi's adventurism. Thus, they accorded Tunisian pleas for increased aid a high priority. Libya's role in orchestrating the attack on Gafsa in 1980 proved that the accusations leveled against Qaddafi had at least some substance. In the wake of the raid, U.S. (and French) naval forces "showed the flag" in Tunisian waters to warn Libya of their support for the Bourguiba government. More important, the United States agreed to Tunisian requests to escalate the already expanding military assistance program by making highly sophisticated weaponry (particularly tanks and fighter aircraft) available to the Tunisian military.

Not all Tunisians thought this approach wise. Critics have argued that these armaments constitute an extravagant and needless expense, claiming that in the event of a full-scale onslaught by Libya (or any other invader), Tunisian forces would still have to depend on quick U.S. or French intervention to hold the attackers at bay. Many Western military analysts agree with this assessment. The reluctance of the United States to condemn the Israeli raid on Tunis in October 1985, even though President Bourguiba had recently visited Washington and received assurances of support for his country's territorial integrity, led many Tunisians to question the value of close ties with the United States. Amid persistent rumors that U.S. intelligence had known of the raid in advance, opponents of close relations between the two countries asserted that the United States might support Tunisia against its own Arab nemesis, Colonel Qaddafi, but proved unwilling to come to Tunisia's defense (militarily or diplomatically) when it was attacked by a power with which the United States enjoyed good relations, Israel. An outburst of anti-U.S. sentiment erupted in the aftermath of the Israeli raid, but officials of both the Tunisian and U.S. governments worked to prevent an open breach.

Pointing to the straitened circumstances of the country's economy, other advocates of Tunisia's distancing itself from the United States have maintained that funds spent on arms purchases were more sorely needed to finance crucial economic and social programs. Opponents of the regime have also expressed concern that weapons ostensibly acquired to defend Tunisia's frontiers might be turned against the PSD's domestic enemies—a concern heightened by the army's growing involvement in repressing antigovernment demonstrations. A final doubt about the advisability of a massive military buildup has revolved around the added economic burdens imposed by the U.S. extension of military credits, which has contributed significantly to raising Tunisia's debt service ratio.

AFRICA

Tunisia's traditional economic and political connections with sub-Saharan Africa deteriorated during the nineteenth century and virtually ended with the establishment of the protectorate. Although few strong ties with that region existed at the time of independence, Tunisia actively participated in the founding of the Organization of African Unity (OAU) in 1963. Bourguiba's record both as a leader in the anticolonial struggle and as a partisan of modernization won him the admiration of many nationalist politicians in French-speaking Africa, some of whom he had known since his student days in France. Bourguiba seconded their demands for independence and urged the growing number of sovereign African states to concentrate their efforts on the same kinds of programs under way in Tunisia in the 1960s.

Subsequent economic and social problems revealed flaws in the Tunisian approach to development, but other African nations continued to study Bourguibist policies, particularly those of the early years of independence, for guidance in their own plans for growth and modernization. Tunisia has striven to improve commercial and political contacts with Africa over the years, but its traditional linkages with the European and Middle Eastern worlds, and the more immediate importance of those areas to Tunisian interests, have led officials to devote less attention to cultivating better ties with the rest of Africa.

NOTES

1. Because the attacks occurred on the anniversary of the Black Thursday riots of 1978 and because Ashur had recently visited Libya, some party loyalists raised questions about UGTT involvement in the Gafsa raid. Ashur, like every other prominent Tunisian, however, condemned the foray.

2. This was an early example of the gap between Tunisia's elites and its future elites, the country's youth. The gap widened during the 1970s, creating the discontent symbolized by the disturbances of 1978, 1980, and 1984.

3. The 1984 figures appear in Richard B. Parker, *North Africa: Regional Tensions and Strategic Concerns* (New York: Praeger, 1984), p. 170. For the earlier statistics, see Robert Santucci, "La politique étrangère de la Tunisie," *Maghreb-Machrek* 91 (January-March 1981):51.

Conclusion

Cultural influences from a variety of areas in the Mediterranean Basin have provided the foundations of modern Tunisia. Throughout its history, Tunisia has acted as a funnel through which outsiders' ideals and values have been introduced into North Africa. From Tunisia new concepts spread to the more remote areas of the Maghrib and across the desert into sub-Saharan Africa. The eastern Mediterranean was one important source of formative influences, beginning with the Phoenicians, who first brought the area actively into the Mediterranean sphere. Even more momentous was the Arab conquest of Mediterranean Africa. The Arabs introduced Islam, which the Berbers readily adopted, and the Arabic language and culture, which they accepted more hesitantly. But the migration of tribes from the Middle East and the close affinity between Islam and the Arabs resulted in the evolution of a society imbued with Arab, as well as Islamic, traits. Eventually, all but minimal traces of the Berber language and customs disappeared, creating a more homogeneous society than anywhere else in the Maghrib.

Despite its links with the lands and people of the eastern Mediterranean, geographical and historical realities led Tunisia to develop an identity of its own, although very much within the broader Arabo-Islamic context. The Aghlabid, Zirid, Hafsid, and preprotectorate Husainid rulers all saw themselves as heads of Muslim states with some attachment to wider Muslim polities. At the same time, all of them assiduously avoided the absorption of their lands into those larger states. The desire for a specific Tunisian identity within the Arabo-Islamic community continues. For example, Tunisia supports the principle of a "Greater Maghrib" but, as the smallest state in the region, carefully guards against efforts by its more powerful neighbors to gain hegemony in the area. The decision to locate the headquarters of the Arab League in Tunisia after 1979 verified the country's place within the Arab world and also took advantage of Tunisia's long-standing ties to the West. Although to a much lesser extent than has occurred with Islam and the Arabs, the culture of Mediterranean Europe has shaped Tunisia's identity.

At several critical historical junctures, the technological superiority and more extensive reserves of human and material resources available to the lands on the northern shores of the Mediterranean enabled them to dominate Tunisia. Rome's defeat of Carthage was the first example of this process. European control of Mediterranean commerce, especially after the Ottoman-Hapsburg wars, was another. But by far the most obvious and most significant was nineteenth- and twentieth-century European colonialism.

The intensity of the colonial experience ensured that its legacy would remain long after the last colon had left Tunisia. Like the people of many territories subjected to European control, Tunisians developed a love-hate relationship with the West even before the formal inauguration of the protectorate. Many of them wanted to introduce to Tunisia features of Western culture, from the high-quality products of its factories, which could be imported more cheaply than the inferior goods produced by local craftspeople, to the political concepts of just and responsible government, which their advocates were certain would strengthen the country and bring it prosperity. Few Tunisians, however, were prepared to discard totally the traditions and customs of the Arabo-Islamic world. Thus, tensions developed between mutually suspicious proponents of sometimes conflicting value systems and approaches to problem solving. Even the struggle to end imperial rule reflected these tensions. The Salafiyya movement heavily influenced the Young Tunisians; the Dustur party glorified an idealized Arabo-Islamic past that had never existed in Tunisia as the party portrayed it; and the Neo-Dustur and, even more so, the Socialist Dustur party incorporated many Western notions in their ideologies. Today, Tunisia not only participates in the Arab League but is also an associate member of the European Economic Community, illustrating its continuing interest in these two divergent cultures. Whatever the future may hold for the country, strands from both the eastern and northern Mediterranean traditions are certain to remain woven into its cultural composition.

The tension between Islamic customs and Western practices is one of many troubling issues in modern Tunisia that has been placed on hold in the currently uncertain political atmosphere. Since President Bourguiba's heart condition worsened in fall 1984, the government has been paralyzed. It has reacted to critical situations as they have arisen but has proved unable to formulate decisive plans for the future owing to rivalries within the inner circle of the party and doubts about positions Bourguiba will take on various issues when and if he resumes his commanding role. Prime Minister Mzali, generally perceived as an advocate of change, cannot risk alientating conservative elements in the PSD and in Bourguiba's family—Mrs. Bourguiba is a formidable ally of the conservatives—capable of influencing the chief executive's thinking. Moreover, the president's behavior in the January 1984 riots showed him willing to undermine other politicians, including Mzali, to retain his own prestige. Consequently, it is unlikely that any significant changes will occur as long as Bourguiba remains alive, despite the pressing need for change revealed by the bloody disturbances of early 1984. Bourguiba's decision to rescind the price hikes precipitating those riots addressed only their superficial causes; virtually none of the root issues of the unrest has been alleviated.

These issues include the stagnant economy and the unrepresentative political system. In late 1984, unofficial Western estimates placed the unemployment rate at or near 30 percent. Many other Tunisians are underemployed. In stark contrast with the large number of people unable to find suitable work, or any work at all, is a class of newly wealthy Tunisians who have reaped enormous profits from speculative ventures and investments in foreign enterprises in the country. It appears likely that the resuscitation of the economy will be a lengthy process requiring austerity measures similar to those recommended by the International Monetary Fund at the end of 1983. Should this be the case, the government will need to find a mechanism in which the heaviest burdens imposed by the belt-tightening do not fall upon the poorest segments of the population—the popular conception of the impact of the decision to withdraw key subsidies in the beginning of 1984. A means must also be found to involve the many disgruntled Tunisians, especially the country's youth, in the political process in a constructive fashion so as to dispel their conviction that the government is unconcerned about their very serious problems.

None of these matters is likely to be addressed adequately in the present political climate. Constitutionally, the prime minister succeeds to the presidency on the death of the incumbent, but where real power will reside in the post-Bourguiba state and precisely how that state will respond to critical domestic and international questions are subjects of pure speculation. Assuming that the constitutional process is followed, any one of several feasible scenarios could unfold. The one seemingly offering the best prospects for solving Tunisia's most acute problems is the formation of a "national unity" government headed by Mzali but including representatives of all existing political organizations as well as of other groups currently banned from participating in politics—most notably the Mouvement de Tendance Islamique. Mzali has already brought a hint of political pluralism to the country by legalizing some parties within rather rigid limits, but any further moves in that direction would probably encounter resistance from old guard PSD leaders. It remains unclear whether Mzali, operating outside the shadow of Bourguiba, would undertake such an opening of the political process, or, if he did, whether he could bring his conservative critics along in the scheme. The tradition of one-party government is a well-embedded article of faith for many of the political elite, and any successful alteration of it, especially in a dramatic fashion, will, at the very least, be a drawn-out process.

In a variation on the political pluralism theme, post-Bourguiba PSD leaders might try to neutralize their most serious rivals by permitting more debate within the party and inviting dissidents to work under the PSD umbrella, emphasizing the party's historic role in the nationalist movement and in bringing about social change after independence. They might argue that the reconstruction of a unified party utilizing the considerable resources of the PSD (especially its well-organized cellular structure) would provide an excellent mechanism for assessing public opinion and for implementing plans agreed on at the highest levels of the party by people representing a variety of views. Such an arrangement would, presumably, make a particular effort to deal with the grievances of those once important parts of the Neo-Dustur coalition, including students and workers, who have lost confidence in the party's ability to deal with Tunisia's troubles. To achieve the desired end, such a process would depend upon the willingness of the entrenched PSD hard-liners to allow (at least up to a point) genuinely opposing views to be heard—a contingency that is by no means certain. This approach would preserve the single-party state, to the satisfaction of conservatives, but might also provide a bridge for an eventual transition to a more truly pluralistic political culture, to the satisfaction of the more liberally minded.

A temporary expansion of political activity after Bourguiba's death, followed by a quick return to authoritarian government, is yet a third possibility. This scenario assumes the inability of reform leaders or moderates to make their counsel prevail within the inner circles of the post-Bourguiba party.

All the prospects noted thus far fall within the range of "normal" politics. Other, more extraordinary, responses to Bourguiba's death, though less likely, should not be ruled out entirely. It is conceivable that one or another of Tunisia's neighbors having significant ideological differences with the country's present government might try to take advantage of the instability certain to follow the president's demise to threaten the new Tunisian leaders with dire consequences if they did not structure the post-Bourguiba state more to its liking. Based on the historical record, the country most likely to pursue such a policy is Libya. But two important considerations minimize the chances of a foreign-imposed government. The first is the strong resistance to such an attempt likely to emerge across the Tunisian political spectrum. The responses of Tunisian politicians to the Gafsa incident indicated the unanimity of opposition to outside intervention, as does the long tradition of preserving a specifically Tunisian identity. Moreover, Tunisia's most important allies have uniformly and unhesitatingly condemned Libyan meddling in the affairs of its neighbors, including Tunisia. There is no reason to suppose that any form of Libyan intervention in Tunisia would not trigger a quick, decisive, and effective response from France and the United States (as they reacted to the Gafsa raid) to preserve the integrity of a strategically important friend in the Mediterranean.

For many years, one of Bourguiba's strongest principles was to keep the military out of politics. This notion conformed with the president's intellectual background but was undoubtedly reinforced in the 1950s and 1960s when the military coup was a common means of altering governments in the Arab world. Recently, however, the Tunisian military has become more politicized, largely because Bourguiba has deviated from his own maxim and has used the army to maintain order in periods of domestic crisis. Many senior officers have become disillusioned with the politicians' inability to cope with the deteriorating political and economic situations—a shortcoming that they hold responsible for their being drawn into the political arena. Should a post-Bourguiba regime, regardless of its composition, prove unable to provide leadership acknowledged by most Tunisians as capable of restoring political stability and ensuring a revival of the economy, military officers might consider it their duty to remove the politicians and impose order themselves. Given the nonpolitical tradition of the armed forces, however, such a step would almost certainly be a last resort and not one that the army would welcome enthusiastically. Were it to occur, a military intervention on the Turkish pattern—with a quick return to the barracks after placing the national house in order—would be most likely.

Another danger, should there be no evidence of meaningful change after Bourguiba's death, is a popular revolution. Despite the violent upheavals Tunisia has experienced since 1978, this consequence seems improbable. Any successor governmernt, even one dominated by the conservative wing of the PSD, can hardly avoid recognizing the need to adjust party policies that clearly lacked popular support

but could not be changed as long as Bourguiba remained alive. Whoever they are, Bourguiba's successors will know that some concessions are necessary, although they may wish to keep those concessions to a minimum. Since none of the mainstream opposition groups has yet advocated total revolution, government willingness to allow some change may be sufficient to check the immediate threat of a violent overthrow of the government, although greater compromises will eventually be needed to eliminate the danger entirely. Because few Tunisian leaders, soldiers or civilians, inside or outside of government, are prepared to express publicly their views on the most desirable structure for the post-Bourguiba state, it is difficult to judge which of these possibilities, or which other ones, are most likely to materialize.

In many respects, the most fundamental question that the post-Bourguiba government will have to face concerns the role of Islam in Tunisia. The Neo-Dustur campaign after independence to keep religion from impinging on the secular sphere called into question Islam's traditional place in Tunisia and created the image of a society placing Western values above Muslim ones. Since then, no country in the Arabo-Islamic world has projected a more westernized and thus less traditionally Islamic image. The beaches of Hammamet and Sousse may be far from representing the essential Tunisia, but they are the image Tunisia has presented to the rest of the world. The apparent official disinterest in Islam lay at the core of the conditions giving rise to the MTI and similar movements.

The Mouvement de Tendance Islamique is a relatively new phenomenon; the Islamic tendency in Tunisia is not. The country's history provides numerous examples of Tunisia's championing Islamic causes: Kharajism in the eighth century, Shiism in the tenth, and the Al-Muwahhid philosophy in the twelfth. The inspiration for the first two came from the Arabo-Islamic heartlands; the third was an indigenous Maghribi concept and was extremely puritanical and conservative. Ifriqiya was also an early bastion of the Maliki madhhab, one of the strictest of the Islamic legal schools. When weak rulers found it impossible to hold European intruders at bay (the Normans in the eleventh century, the Spaniards in the fifteenth and sixteenth), resistance often rallied around religious figures, and when Tunisians could not handle the burden of defense themselves, they sought help from the greatest Muslim power of the day, the Ottoman Empire.

Although many observers might dismiss these events as ancient history and of no relevance to the present situation, they undoubtedly helped to form Tunisian attitudes about Islam and its place in the society. The prolonged contact with the West, even during the colonial period when it was at its most intense, did not—indeed could not—

eradicate or supplant the imprint that the many earlier centuries of Islamic cultural dominance had left on the country. Islam was as important to the Tunisian masses after the protectorate as before it; perhaps it was more important. The religious, political, and social ideas of Islamic reformers like Muhammad Abduh inspired the earliest opposition to the methods of the protectorate, just as similar ideas about the Islamic community had earlier inspired Khair-al-Din and would later inspire the founders of the Dustur. In the 1930s, even after the political triumph of the westernized Neo-Dusturians, a movement of Islamic reform patterned on and loosely associated with the more famous Algerian Association of Ulama continued to operate in Tunisia. The Neo-Dustur, with its broad support and effective organization, soon overshadowed groups whose views did not coincide with its own. Because the history and traditions of the nationalist struggle have been preserved primarily by the Neo-Dusturians who have controlled the postindependence government, the activities of individuals and groups not affiliated with the Neo-Dustur have been minimized. This statement does not suggest that the party was not the driving force behind Tunisian nationalism and the main determinant of the shape of the modern state: Clearly it was. It rather asserts that other tendencies, and particularly an Islamic one, were always present.

Although the impact on modern Tunisia of liberal nationalism, trade unionism, and other Western-derived philosophies must not be underestimated, a strong and steady current of Islamic feeling has always been present in the country and is likely to come to the surface in whatever kind of political restructuring occurs after Bourguiba's death. In all probability, Islam will neither dominate the post-Bourguiba state nor be pushed aside and subordinated to the extent that it has been since independence. Considering the strong pulls in Tunisia of both East and West, it may be possible that an accommodation can be reached in which the late twentieth-century Islamic revival and the Western liberal tradition coexist. In view of the country's heritage, perhaps it is not too much to hope that in Tunisia the West will learn to live with Islam more easily and with less fear.

Glossary of Foreign Words

(A)=Arabic, (F)=French, (L)=Latin, (T)=Turkish

agha (T)	military rank; commander
Ahl al-kitab (A)	"People of the Book"; Christians and Jews who, like the Muslims, had books of revealed Scriptures
amir (A)	prince
amir al-muminin (A)	"Commander of the Faithful"; title of the caliph, Muhammad's successor as spiritual and temporal head of the Muslim community
bey (T)	military rank; title accorded to Tunisian rulers of the Husainid Dynasty (1705–1957)
bidonville (F)	shanty town
circonscription (F)	administrative subdivision
colon (F)	settler
contrôleur civil (F)	local French administrator of the protectorate
département (F)	province
dey (T)	military rank
diwan (A and T)	administrative council; cabinet
fallaqa (A)	"bandits"; members of the militant resistance to France at close of the protectorate era
funduq (A)	hostel and warehouse for European merchants
habus (A)	pious endowment; land the revenue of which is set aside for religious or charitable purposes
imam (A)	prayer leader; by extension leader of the Muslim community, the caliph
iqta (A)	land grant

179

jihad (A)   "struggle"; defense of the Islamic community
                     and its values
kouloughli (T)   persons of mixed Arab-Turkish ancestry
latifundia (L)   large agricultural estates
madhhab (A)   Muslim legal school
mahalla (A)   military expedition, especially one to raise
                     taxes and "show the flag" in the Tunisian
                     interior
mahdi (A)   "rightly guided one"; Messianic figure who
                     will restore the purity of the original
                     Muslim community
majba (A)   capitation tax
maluf (A)   Tunisian popular music of Andalusian origin
mamluk (A)   slaves of the royal family trained to serve in
                     administrative and military positions for the
                     state
pasha (T)   honorific title applied to Ottoman provincial
                     governors
praetor (L)   Roman administrative official; magistrate
qadi (A)   judge in an Islamic court
qaid (A)   provincial governor; head of a tribal
                     confederation
ribat (A)   fortified mosque, usually part of coastal
                     defense system
sharia (A)   Muslim law
shashiya (A)   red brimless headgear of male Tunisian
                     Muslims
ulama (A)   plural form of *alim*, religious scholar

Selected Bibliography

The pre-Islamic and modern (nineteenth- and twentieth-century) eras are the only phases of Tunisian history well covered by books in English. Even for these periods, however, the bulk of the material is in French and, increasingly, Arabic. This bibliography focuses on works in English, listing only a few of the most important studies in French. Several English-language overviews on North Africa featuring useful chapters on Tunisia are also included.

BOOKS

Abun-Nasr, Jamil. *A History of the Maghrib*. 2d ed. Cambridge: Cambridge University Press, 1975.

Allman, James. *Social Mobility, Education, and Development in Tunisia*. Leiden: Brill, 1979.

Bachrouch, Taoufik. *Les Barbaresques de Tunisie au XVIIè siècle: mythes et interprétations*. Tunis: Université de Tunis, 1977.

Bdira, Mezri. *Relations internationales et sous-développement: la Tunisie, 1857–1864*. Stockholm: Almqvist and Wiksell, 1978.

Beling, Willard. *Modernization and African Labor: A Tunisian Case Study*. New York: Praeger, 1965.

Braudel, Fernand. *The Mediterranean and the Mediterranean World in the Age of Philip II*. 2 vols. New York: Harper and Row, 1973.

Broughton, T.R.S. *The Romanization of Africa Proconsularis*. Baltimore: Johns Hopkins University Press, 1929.

Brown, L. Carl. *The Tunisia of Ahmad Bey*. Princeton: Princeton University Press, 1974.

Brunschvig, Robert. *La Barbérie orientale sous les Hafsides des origines à la fin du XVè siècle*. 2 vols. Paris: Adrien-Maisonneuve, 1940, 1947.

Courtois, Christian. *Les Vandales et l'Afrique*. Paris: Arts et métiers graphiques, 1955.

Diehl, Charles, *L'Afrique Byzantine. Histoire de la domination byzantine en Afrique*. 2 vols. Paris: E. Leroux, 1896.

Duvignaud, Jean. *Change at Shebika*. New York: Pantheon, 1970.

Frend, W.H.C. *The Donatist Church*. Oxford: Clarendon Press, 1952.

Gallagher, Charles F. *The United States and North Africa*. Cambridge, Mass.: Harvard University Press, 1967.

Gallagher, Nancy. *Medicine and Power in Tunisia*. Cambridge: Cambridge University Press, 1983.

Ganiage, Jean. *Les Origines du protectorat français en Tunisie (1861–1881)*. Paris: Presses Universitaires de France, 1959.

Green, Arnold. *The Tunisian Ulama, 1873–1915: Social Structure and Response to Ideological Currents*. Leiden: Brill, 1978.

Idris, Hady Roger. *La Berbérie orientale sous les Zirides, Xè-XIIè siècles*. 2 vols. Paris: Adrien-Maisonneuve, 1962.

Julien, Charles-André. *History of North Africa*. London: Routledge and Kegan Paul, 1970.

———. *L'Afrique du nord en marche: nationalismes musulmanes et souveraineté français*. Paris: Julliard, 1972.

Khair al-Din al-Tunisi. *The Surest Path*. Cambridge, Mass.: Harvard University Press, 1967.

Lawless, Richard, and Allan Findlay, eds. *North Africa: Contemporary Politics and Economic Development*. London: Croom Helm, 1984.

Le Tourneau, Roger. *L'Evolution politique de l'Afrique du nord musulmane, 1920–1961*. Paris: Armand Colin, 1962.

Ling, Dwight. *Tunisia: From Protectorate to Republic*. Bloomington, Ind.: Indiana University Press, 1967.

Marçais, Georges. *La Berbérie musulmane et l'Orient au moyen age*. Paris: Aubier, 1946.

Marsden, Arthur. *British Diplomacy and Tunis: 1875–1902*. Edinburgh: Scottish Academic Press, 1971.

Micaud, Charles, L. Carl Brown, and Clement Henry Moore. *Tunisia: The Politics of Modernization*. New York: Praeger, 1964.

Moore, Clement Henry. *Tunisia Since Independence*. Berkeley: University of California Press, 1965.

O'Donnell, Joseph D. *Lavigerie in Tunisia: The Interplay of Imperialist and Missionary*. Athens, Georgia: University of Georgia Press, 1979.

Parker, Richard. *North Africa: Regional Tensions and Strategic Concerns*. New York: Praeger, 1984.

Rudebeck, Lars. *Party and People: A Study of Political Change in Tunisia*. Stockholm: Almqvist and Wiksell, 1967.

Salem, Norma. *Habib Bourguiba, Islam, and the Creation of Tunisia.* London: Croom Helm, 1984.

Slama, Bice. *L'Insurrection de 1864 en Tunisie.* Tunis: Maison Tunisienne de l'Edition, 1967.

Stone, Russell A., and John Simmons. *Change in Tunisia: Studies in the Social Sciences.* Albany: State University of New York Press, 1976.

Talbi, Mohamed. *L'Emirat aghlabide, 800–909: Histoire politique.* Paris: Adrien-Maisonneuve, 1966.

Valensi, Lucette. *On the Eve of Colonialism. North Africa Before the French Conquest, 1790–1830.* New York: Africana, 1977.

Warmington, B. H. *Carthage.* London: R. Hale, 1960.

————. *The North African Provinces from Diocletian to the Vandal Conquest.* Cambridge: Cambridge University Press, 1954.

Zartman, I. William, ed. *Political Elites in Arab North Africa.* New York: Longman, 1982.

Ziadeh, Nicola. *Origins of Nationalism in Tunisia.* Beirut: American University of Beirut Press, 1962.

JOURNALS

A number of scholarly journals frequently include articles on Tunisia. Among the most important are

Cahiers de Tunisie	(Tunis)
International Journal of Middle East Studies	(Cambridge)
Maghreb-Machrek	(Paris)
Maghreb Review	(London)
Middle East Journal	(Washington)
Revue d'Histoire Maghrébine	(Tunis)
Revue de l'Institut des Belles Lettres Arabes (IBLA)	(Tunis)
Revue de l'Occident Musulman et de la Méditerranée	(Aix-en-Provence)

A weekly newsmagazine in French with good coverage of contemporary political and economic issues in Tunisia is *Jeune Afrique* (Paris).

Index

Names and terms beginning with the Arabic definite article (al-) are indexed under the letter following the article. An article in the middle of a name or term is treated as part of the word.